SEARCH FOR SILENCE

Where shall the word be found, where will the word
Resound? Not here, there is not enough silence

T.S. Eliot
"Ash Wednesday"

SEARCH FOR SILENCE

Revised Edition

by Elizabeth O'Connor

Foreword by N. Gordon Cosby
The Church of The Saviour
Washington, D.C.

San Diego, California

LuraMedia™

Publisher's Catalog Number LM-604
Printed and Bound in the United States of America

LuraMedia™
10227 Autumnview Lane
P. O. Box 261668
San Diego, California 92126-0998

Library of Congress Cataloging-in-Publication Data

O'Connor, Elizabeth.
  Search for silence.

  Bibliography: p.
  1. Contemplation.   2. Devotional exercises.
I. Title.
BV5091.C7027   1986   248.3   86-114
ISBN 0-931055-07-5

To
Dorothy Ham Devers
faithful friend of hidden ministries
whose name has always been written
on this book

A WORD ABOUT LANGUAGE

As a publisher LuraMedia™ is committed to the use of inclusive language. However, changing the wording of quotations from other sources is beyond the scope of our influence. As a result, the quotations in this book from the Revised Standard Version of the Bible, The New English Bible, and The Jerusalem Bible, as well as the numerous other selected readings, do not reflect our language position. We have made every attempt to insure the accuracy of each quotation, and we entrust the reader with the task of expanding the reference of any restrictive pronouns.

CONTENTS

FOREWORD

The one journey that ultimately matters is the journey into the place of stillness deep within one's self. To reach that place is to be at home; to fail to reach it is to be forever restless. At the place of "central silence," one's own life and spirit are united with the life and Spirit of God. There the fire of God's presence is experienced. The soul is immersed in love. The divine birth happens. We hear at last the living Word. Meister Eckhart reminds us that a wise man said, "When all things lay in the midst of silence then leapt there down into me from on high, from the royal throne, a secret word" (Wisdom 18:14). The secret Word is heard in a place of inward silence. Out of a profound understanding of the urgent need to hear and heed that Word, *Search for Silence* was written.

God's transcendent mystery is everywhere in the universe— above us, beneath us, in us, through us. The contemplative is the one who perceives the mystery, a perception that is possible for very ordinary people. Scripture says matter-of-factly, "Enoch walked with God." I believe that such a walk is possible for each of us. This is the promise that breathes through *Search for Silence*. The same message is found in the Old Testament and in the New Testament. We hear it sounded in God's words to Moses, "I shall be with you" (Ex. 3:14), and we hold, if ever so wistfully, in our hearts these words, "and they will call him Immanuel, a name which means 'God-is-with-us' " (Matt. 1:23, *Jer.*).

In our deepest beings we are all contemplatives. We glimpse what this means in times when we have surrendered ourselves to a piece of work and the hours seem as moments. We are contemplatives when we are absorbed by an experience of love, beauty, wonder, grief, or when we are able to be present to something or someone with the totality of ourselves. These occasions, however, are more rare than need be. The fact is that very few of us know how to pray, though our very beings are coded for praying. We do not know who we are, and we do not know God. The call to prayer is a call to become aware of our true selves and a call to an intimate relationship with God. Out of this relationship we are empowered to say to others what every heart yearns to hear, "I shall be with you." The person who can say, "I saw the Lord high and lifted up" (Isaiah 2:1, *RSV*) is the person on whom others can rely. The person who can say "I know where I came from and where I am going" (John 8:14, *Jer.*) is a free person.

The contemplative is on the journey to wholeness, autonomy, freedom — the freedom to love, to care, to transfigure the earth. Ultimately contemplation is related to our vocation — to what we are to do in the world. God gives us not only an incomplete self; God gives us an incomplete world. In contemplative prayer we participate in God's nature, we are in touch with our own divinity. Latent creative powers in us become alive.

God does not act in a vacuum. God, our mother, our father, acts in a covenant relationship with each of us. The terrible, wonderful truth is that God's existence in the world is dependent on us, as our existence is dependent on God. Not long before she died in the gas chambers of Auschwitz, 29-year old Etty Hillesum prayed:

> Dear God, these are anxious times. Tonight for the first time I lay in the dark with burning eyes as scene after scene of human suffering passed before me. I shall promise You one thing, God, just one very small thing: I shall never burden my today with cares about my tomorrow, although that takes some practice. Each day is sufficient unto itself. I shall try to help You, God, to stop my strength ebbing away, though I cannot vouch for it in advance. But one thing is becoming increasingly clear to me: that You cannot help us, that we must help You to help ourselves. And that is all we can manage these days and also all that really matters: that we safeguard that little piece of You, God, in ourselves. And perhaps in others as well. Alas, there doesn't seem to be much You Yourself can do about our circumstances, about our lives. Neither do I hold You responsible. You cannot help us but we must help You and defend Your dwelling place inside us to the last . . .[1]

We call to God, God calls to us. We wait on God, and God waits on us. In Scripture is the plaintive voice of God, "I called and you would not answer, I spoke and you would not listen" (Isaiah 65:12, *Jer.*). I doubt very much that there is any creativity in the world apart from contemplation. In contemplation we catch a vision of not only what is, but what can be. We find our place in salvation history.

Contrary to what we have thought, contemplatives are the great doers. Contemplatives return from times of withdrawal with inner clarity and with direction. In their return from the silence they take up the work of giving form to the liberating truths that have been given to them in flashes of insight and vision. They are also the great enablers of others. They evoke spirit in those they meet. Because they have been present to themselves, they are able to be present to others in a way that awakens, enlivens, gives courage. In them we see more clearly a way of existence that combines both being and doing.

Search for Silence is a guide book, drawn from the literature of contemplative prayer, for those who would like to be on the most extraordinary of all journeys. We live in a time when more and more adventurers will be making flights to the moon. These ascents into outer space fill us with awe, as well they may, but they are not comparable to the ascent to God which Elizabeth O'Connor urges us to make by plunging into the depths of our own lives.

Part One of *Search for Silence* deals with confession which enables us to reach an inward place of silence. When we withdraw from our usual occupations and try to settle down, we find it hard to sit still, we are restless and ill at ease. Our task is to acknowledge these feelings, to meditate on them, and try to discover what they have to tell us. With time to listen and to reflect, we will awake to what is in our hearts — all those feelings that in the rush of our days we keep hidden from ourselves and from others. Silence will put us in touch with yearnings, anxieties, pain, despair, envy, competition, and a host of other feelings that need to be put into words if we are to move toward a place of centeredness and come into possession of our lives. The fact is that most of us have an incredible amount of unfaced suffering in our histories that has to be looked at and worked through.

Confession has to do with facing and naming before God the darkness within us — crying out the grief that has marked us and too often been covered over. Confession also has to do with naming before God the light within us — being willing to confess our gifts even when that means becoming responsible for them. The God who speaks in the depths of our beings always bids us reach into the world of the unconscious, so that we may bring into the world of consciousness more of our real selves. Without a preparatory time of confession each day, no real silence is possible, nor is any new vision given.

Part Two of *Search for Silence* will give the reader specific help in following the contemplative way. The author places the section on contemplative prayer within the context of a coffee house — The Potter's House — to illustrate how contemplation and action intersect and become one.

The Potter's House was one of the first corporate efforts of The Church of The Saviour in Washington, D.C. Most of us were engaged in individual outreach and occasional group projects, but we had not fully developed servant structures that would enable each member to be on corporate mission. To help us in our quest for new wineskins we formed classes in Christian Vocation. In these classes we took a deeper and longer look at the whole matter of call as having to do with the transcendent. We began with the basic assumption of the New Testament that there is no way to be the church except by the call of Christ. Elizabeth O'Connor outlined some of the dimensions of this call as follows:

> *First*, it is a call to become persons in a relationship with God as intimate as the one which Christ knew.
>
> *Second*, it is a call to become persons in community with others responding to the same call, surrendering something of our own authority that we might have a shared life and bring into existence a new community where the nature of relationships will enable each person to be called fully into being.
>
> *Third*, it is a call to an inward development — a call to change. We are to overcome those obstacles in ourselves which hold us back and keep us from growing up into the full stature of Christ. The call of Christ is a call to die to the old self in order to become the new creation.
>
> *Fourth*, and not last, it is a call to move out — to discover where we are to lay down our lives — to take up the stance of the suffering servant and make witness to the power of Jesus Christ at work in us.

In the classes on Vocation we worked primarily with the fourth dimension of call. If the church is a sent people, where was Christ sending each of us? To what segment of the world's need were we to make response? We began each class session by sitting for an hour in the silence, knowing that if any word was to be addressed to us we had more opportunity of hearing it in the stillness of our own souls. The primary work of each hour was to center deeply enough in ourselves to be in touch with our own most central wish. We had then, as we have now, the conviction that our wishes lie very close to "who we are" and what we are to be doing. To commune with one's inmost self is to have a sense of being dealt with by the One who is Other.

Despite our expectancy, no one in this class was addressed by a Voice, which is the meaning of "hearing call." We learned in those days that God does not descend out of heaven and summon us as we sit with heads bowed. God comes to most of us through the commonplace events of life, which become *extraordinary* events because out of our time in the silence we bring to the ordinary a deepened sensitivity and a new quality of seeing and hearing.

Halfway through the class one of those ordinary, but *extraordinary,* events occurred. My wife, Mary, and I were in New England where I gave a Lenten sermon at a large church. The setting was formal; the people elegantly dressed; the spirit frigid. I preached to the limit of my vision on the intensity of Christ's love for us. The emotional and spiritual climate did not change.

We left the church that night with discouraged spirits and drove to the next town. At a small hotel we were given the last vacant room, which was above the tavern. The noise of the juke box and the celebrating people below made it difficult to sleep. At first we were irritated, but the vibrant voices and gay melodies made us reflect that Jesus would probably be more at home in the tavern than in the church we had left.

The next morning we had breakfast at a small coffee house close to the hotel. The people who went in and out greeted one another, read their newspapers, and commented on the day's news. Again we had time to reflect that Christ would be more at home in the coffee house than in the church we had visited.

I went home and told the class on Christian Vocation that I would like to find a way to take the church to the restaurants of the city. Out of the dialogue that night emerged the idea of a coffee house. I knew that I had heard call. In the next weeks I was able to communicate it to others in such a way that it came as "Good News" to them. About twelve of us began to search for suitable quarters. After a long time of looking and praying for the gift of discernment, that small group of called people found and rented a vacant store. Soon after began the work of renovation that would turn a large and ugly room into a center of beauty and creativity.

As we watched the transformation take place we knew that prayer would be the foundation of this and every other mission of The Church of The Saviour. The disciplines for members and intern members in mission groups were hammered out, and within a short time there were eight or ten people to staff each of the nights, and thus each night had what we have come to call a "mission group." From the beginning the disciplines of these groups included "daily solitude, prayer, and Scripture study." One year when we felt on a long desert stretch we appointed Elizabeth O'Connor spiritual director of all the mission groups and asked her to give us some structure for the time each evening, before The Potter's House opened, when the groups met for corporate prayer and study. The exercises in this book were developed by Elizabeth at that time to deepen our belonging to Christ and to one another, and to the segment of the city where we had been placed.

The meditations have served us and other groups ever since. They have been our Ignatian Exercises. They have sustained and enabled us to endure in times of darkness and tribulation. They gave us practice in serious prayer, which more than any factor has made The Potter's House the seedbed for a cluster of missions that now permeate the neighborhood. Around the tables of The Potter's House, Jubilee Housing came into being to provide safe and affordable space to low-income families. This mission in turn spawned other missions so that today Jubilee has a wholistic ministry to the needs of tenants living in eight Jubilee apartment houses in the surrounding area. Next door to The Potter's House is the Columbia Road Health Services which provides low-cost medical care, and a ministry of intercessory prayer. Presently members of this mission are exploring spiritual healing and prayer for the community at large. Behind The Potter's House is Sarah's Circle, an intergenerational community for the elderly poor. Sarah's Circle is offering hope and choices for a group traditionally denied both. Further down the street from The Potter's House is the Five Loaves Bakery, which makes available job training opportunities for neighborhood persons. Across the street is Jubilee Jobs which finds work for those living in the neighborhood. Nearby is The Family Place serving young mothers and their babies, many of whom are refugees. As I write this, Christ House with an infirmary for street persons is about to open. Soon after that the first Samaritan Inn, giving longer term housing to homeless persons, will receive its first residents.

In the midst of the above, music, poetry, drama and the visual arts abound. When I reflect on all that is unfolding in The Potter's House and other communities of The Church of The Saviour, I am reminded to guard myself against letting the demands that come with these missions tempt me away from the work of prayer. I give thanks that early were engraved on my heart the words of a monk who warned that devotion produces discipline; discipline produces abundance; abundance tends to destroy devotion and discipline.

Search for Silence may be read in two ways. One is to read it simply for the enrichment and inspiration of being in touch with the writers who confirm one's own intimations of a Kingdom within. For some this will be the better way, especially for the first reading. The other choice is to read the book slowly, meditating on the selections and working with the suggested exercises.

If you choose the second way, you will be beginning or continuing an arduous journey Each day allot time for meditation on several of the passages that follow the exercise you are doing. They will give you the help and encouragement needed to reach your own quiet center. You will be tempted a thousand times to forget that Christ called you to make the pilgrimage. But one day you will touch the Silence and understand and exclaim with an unknown preacher,

> See for yourselves how little were my labours compared with the great peace I have found.
> —Ecclestiasticus 51:27, *NEB*

N. Gordon Cosby
The Church of The Saviour
Washington, D.C.

ACKNOWLEDGMENTS

Grateful acknowledgment is made to the following copyright holders for permission to use their copyrighted material:

Georges Borchardt, Inc., (U.S. Agent for Editions du Seuil) for the quotations from INCOGNITO by Petru Dumitriu.

Burns & Oates Ltd., for the quotation from ON PRAYER by Karl Rahner.

Christianity and Crisis, for the quotation from "The Vision of Cesar Chavez" (Jan. 11, 1971) by Glen Gersmehl.

Christian Publications (Camp Hill, Pennsylvania), for the quotation from THE PURSUIT OF GOD by A. W. Tozer.

Citadel Press/Lyle Stuart, Inc., for the quotation from THE WAY OF MAN by Martin Buber.

Commonweal, for the quotation from "Generation without Fathers" (June 12, 1970) by Henry Nouwen.

The Crown Publishing Group, for the quotation reprinted from THE SYMBOLIC AND THE REAL by Ira Progoff. Copyright ©1963 by Ira Progoff. Used by permission of The Julian Press, Inc.

Curtis Brown, Ltd., for the quotation from IMAGES OF HOPE, ©1965 by William F. Lynch, F.J. Used by permission of Curtis Brown, Ltd.

Delacorte Press, for the excerpt from the book THE MASTER GAME by Robert S. de Ropp. Copyright ©1968 by Robert S. de Ropp. Reprinted by permission of Delacorte Press/Seymour Lawrence.

Dodd, Mead & Company, Inc., for the quotation from NORTH WITH THE SPRING by Edwin Way Teale.

Doubleday & Company, Inc., for the quotations from THE JERUSALEM BIBLE, copyright ©1966 by Darton, Longman & Todd, Ltd. and Doubleday & Company, Inc. Reprinted by permission of the publisher.

E. P. Dutton, for the following quotations:
From MYSTICISM by Evelyn Underhill. Published, 1961, in the United States by E. P. Dutton. All rights reserved. Reprinted by permission of the publisher, E. P. Dutton, a division of New American Library.
From PRACTICAL MYSTICISM by Evelyn Underhill. Copyright 1915 by E. P. Dutton, renewed 1943 by Evelyn Underhill. Reprinted by permission of the publisher, E. P. Dutton, a division of New American Library.
Element Books Ltd., for the following quotations:
From CONCENTRATION AND MEDITATION by Christmas Humphreys.
From MEISTER ECKHART, VOL. I, by Meister Eckhart, translated by D. de B. Evans.
Reprinted by permission of the publisher, Element Books Ltd., Longmead, Shaftesbury, Dorset SP7 8PL, England.
Forward Movement Publications, for the quotations from BROTHER LAWRENCE: THE PRACTICE OF THE PRESENCE OF GOD. Forward Movement Publications, 412 Sycamore Street, Cincinnati, Ohio 45202. Used by permission.
The Friends Tract Association, for the quotation from the pamphlet "The Gathered Meeting" by Thomas Kelly.
Fortress Press, for the quotation from HOW THE WORLD BEGAN by Helmut Thielicke.
The Reverend Charles Bartruff Hanna, for the quotations from FACE OF THE DEEP by Charles Hanna.
Harcourt Brace Jovanovich, Inc., for the following excerpts:
From "The Hidden Teacher," copyright ©1964 by Loren Eiseley. Reprinted from his volume THE UNEXPECTED UNIVERSE by permission of Harcourt Brace Jovanovich, Inc.
From "The Cocktail Party," copyright 1950 by T.S. Eliot; renewed 1978 by Esme Valerie Eliot. Reprinted by permission of Harcourt Brace Jovanovich, Inc.
From "Ash Wednesday" in COLLECTED POEMS 1909-1962 by T.S. Eliot, copyright 1936 by Harcourt Brace Jovanovich, Inc., copyright ©1963, 1964 by T. S. Eliot. Reprinted by permission of the pubisher.
From THE WAY OF INDIVIDUATION by Jolande Jacobi, translated by R.F.C. Hull, copyright©1965 by Rascher & Cie, AG, Zurich; English translation copyright ©1967 by Harcourt Brace Jovanovich, Inc. Reprinted by permission of Harcourt Brace Jovanovich, Inc.
Harper & Row, Publishers, Inc., for the following quotations:
From pp. 27, 116 in LIFE TOGETHER by Dietrich Bonhoeffer, Translated by John W. Doberstein. Copyright 1954 by Harper & Row, Publishers, Inc.
From pp. 53-54 "The Creative Attitude" by Erich Fromm, in CREATIVITY AND ITS CULTIVATION, edited by Harold H. Anderson et al. Copyright ©1959 by Harper & Row, Publishers, Inc.
From pp. 50-51 PURITY OF HEART by Soren Kierkegaard, Translated by Douglas V. Steere. Copyright 1938 by Harper & Row, Publishers, Inc.
From p. 89 in THINK ON THESE THINGS by J. Krishnamurti, Edited by D. Rajagopal. Copyright ©1964 by K & R Foundation.
From pp. 34-35 MYSTICISM: CHRISTIAN AND BUDDHIST by D. T. Suzuki. Copyright ©1957 by Daisetz Teitaro Suzuki.
Specified extracts from DIETRICH BONHOEFFER: MAN OF VISION, MAN OF COURAGE by Eberhard Bethge. Copyright ©1967 by Chr. Kaiser Verlag Munchen. English Translation Copyright ©1970 by William Collins Sons & Co.,

Random House, Inc., for the following excerpts:

From IF IT DIE by Andre Gide, translated by Dorothy Bussy. Copyright 1935 and renewed 1963 by Random House, Inc. Reprinted by permission of the publisher.

From PRAYER IN PRACTICE by Romano Guardini, translated by Prince Leopold, Copyright ©1957 by Pantheon Books, a division of Random House, Inc.

From AN INTERRUPTED LIFE — THE DIARIES OF ETTY HILLESUM, 1942-1943, by Etty Hillesum, translated by Arno Pomerans. Copyright ©1983 by Jonathan Cape, Ltd. Reprinted by permission of Pantheon Books, a division of Random House, Inc.

From REMEMBRANCE OF THINGS PAST by Marcel Proust, translated by C. K. Scott Moncrieff and Terence Kilmartin. Copyright ©1981 by Random House, Inc. and Chatto and Windus Ltd. Reprinted by permission of the publisher.

Schocken Books Inc., for the following quotations:

From TEN RUNGS: HASIDIC SAYINGS by Martin Buber. Copyright ©1947 by Schocken Books Inc. Copyright renewed.

From TALES OF THE HASIDIM: EARLY MASTERS by Martin Buber. Copyright ©1947, 1975 by Schocken Books Inc.

From TALES OF THE HASIDIM: LATER MASTERS by Martin Buber. Copyright ©1948 by Schocken Books Inc. Copyright renewed.

Charles Scribner's Sons, for the excerpts from PSYCHOTHERAPY AND A CHRISTIAN VIEW OF MAN by Dr. David E. Roberts. Copyright ©1950 Charles Scribner's Sons; copyright renewed 1978 Elinor N. Roberts. Reprinted with the permission of Charles Scribner's Sons.

Sheed & Ward Ltd., for the quotation from THE COMPLETE WORKS OF ST. TERESA OF JESUS, Vol. I, *Life,* translated and edited by E. Allison Peers, published by Sheed and Ward Ltd.

The Society for Promoting Christian Knowledge (S.P.C.K.), for the quotation from THE USE OF SILENCE by Geoffrey Hoyland.

Spring Publications, Inc. for the quotation from AN INTRODUCTION TO THE INTERPRETATION OF FAIRY TALES by Marie-Louise von Franz (Dallas: Spring Publications, Inc., 1970), p. 76.

The Sterling Lord Agency, Inc., for the quotation from SELF-RENEWAL by John W. Gardner. Reprinted by permission of The Sterling Lord Agency, Inc. ©1981.

TAN Books & Publications, Inc., for the quotation from CONVERSATION WITH CHRIST by Peter-Thomas Rohrbach, O.C.D.

Van Nostrand Reinhold Company, Inc., for the following quotations:

From CREATIVITY AND CONFORMITY by Clark Moustakas, copyright ©Clark Moustakas 1967.

From TOWARD A PSYCHOLOGY OF BEING by Abraham H. Maslow, copyright ©1968 by Litton Educational Publishing Inc., reprinted by permission of Van Nostrand Reinhold Company.

The Westminster Press, for the quotation from THE SCHOOL OF PRAYER by Olive Wyon.

Winston Press, for the quotation from THE WAY OF THE WOLF, ©1968, 69, 70 by Martin Bell. Published by Winston · Seabury Press, Minneapolis, MN. All rights reserved. Used with permission.

CONFESSING OUR HUMANITY

CONFESSING OUR HUMANITY

FEAR

A number of years ago I took a memorable class entitled, "How to Keep One's Own Journal." In the first session we were asked to list our fears and to indicate the one which filled us with the most dread. On my long list I put a circle around the fear that "one day I will be left alone." This was my most private fear. I had no intention of admitting it to anyone.

Connected with my fear was a shame that was not easily put into words. I had the feeling that if I said it aloud, the world would label me an unsuccessful human being, and in the corridors and on the streets people would whisper, "There goes a lonely person." Some might say, "How sad," and ask me to dinner; and I would go, knowing that when all the dinners were over, my fear would still be there, for my fear was projected upon an unknown future when I would, indeed, be alone.

At the next session of the class, it was suggested that those who cared to might say what they had named as their pet fear.

"Being alone," said one person simply. "Being old and alone."

"I have that fear, too," said another. "It is the fear of being abandoned."

"My fear is almost like that," said a third person. "I'm afraid of committing myself to anything, because I'm afraid that somewhere along the way, everyone will fall out, and I'll be left shouldering the whole load."

During those few minutes my outcast fear had grown respectable. It had been described by strong people living not only in the midst of plenty, but in the safety of families. I could say, "Mine, too, is the fear that I shall be left alone."

Only one other fear was named that night — the fear of failure. When we considered this, it also turned out to be the fear of being alone. With failure came the terrible possibility of being cut off from friends.

The evening ended with a period of structured meditation in which we were asked to imagine this scene:

> You have been following Jesus for several days. Even though you have heard him say, "Do not be anxious about tomorrow," "The hairs of your head are all numbered" and "I am with you always," you have kept your own persistent fears. You edge your way through the crowd until you are near enough to Jesus to make a bold petition for a few minutes of his time so that you might say, "I believe; help my unbelief." He nods "yes" to your request and motions you to follow him to a place apart. You sit there beside him on the grass, and he waits for you to speak.

We were then told to write in our notebooks what we imagined we had said to Jesus and what he answered.

That journaling class was a time when we were peculiarly aware that God was with us, that God listened and replied. Unexpectedly we had stumbled on what it means to gather in God's name.

Since then I have pondered the meaning of confession. It was the act of confession that night, binding us together in a community of caring, which released the healing power that needs to be experienced again and again in the process of being made whole. We shared not only the casual things that we were used to sharing, but we also shared some thoughts that were born in the solitary places of our lives when no one else was looking. We dared to say for our own hearing, as well as for the hearing of others, "This is my fear." The illusion of being alone in "fear and trembling" was dispelled. We moved into a sense of oneness that was based on the awareness of our common plight.

For me, that night was the beginning of a long journey in the understanding of a fear. Others, by their confession, had not alienated me, but had tapped strains of caring that made me want to reach out and say to each in turn, "Have no fear." Moreover, I caught a glimpse of the sin of my own pride. It had wrought an unreal image of a self-contained person and would not let that image go.

This is what happens with false imaginings about ourselves. We come to believe more and more in them. We fashion an unreal self and become enmeshed in the nets of our own labor. It does not take long to begin to think that this self — this idol that we have constructed — is all there is to us. We invent our own legend and come to believe that our salvation lies in perpetuating it. This cuts us off from our real self and gives rise to uneasy, tremulous feelings. The fear that hangs suspended like a knife over the future is not so foolish or unexplainable as we think. It turns out to be the prophet of our own soul warning us that the path we are following leads to destruction. It is Jeremiah come back again:

> every goldsmith is put to shame by his idols;
> for his images are false,
>   and there is no breath in them.
> They are worthless, a work of delusion . . .
>   they shall perish.
> —Jeremiah 10:14-15, *RSV*

Our inner prophets are often bold to say that a Kingdom is coming before which all false images will topple and crash; but we must do more than tremble before signs and prophecies. Something more is required. We must give up our illusions about the kind of people we are. We are not going to do this, however, unless we have come to believe that beneath the unreal facade there exists another self that can indeed breathe and live. We do not give up false concepts without at least the beginnings of faith in an unseen, imperishable Kingdom within. Confession starts us on the journey toward that lost Kingdom.

But we did more the night of our journaling class than place our fears in an arena where we might more fully confront them. In the end we put them down at the feet of the One who has the power to say not only, "Have no fear," but also, "I am with you always, even to the end of the world." On that night I heard those words from another level of being. Perhaps it was because I had begun to believe a little more in the availability of my own love. In spite of all my human frailty, those same words had been so formed in me that I might have spoken them to others: "Have no fear . . ." If I, being human, knew how to give good gifts, how much more so the one I call Lord and God?

LONELINESS

To find loneliness under the heading of confession is probably unusual, but this is where it belongs. My fears and longings begin to tell you who I am and how I hope and suffer. Always it is hard to confess this part of me, for each time involves new risk. In my clumsiness (or in my reserve), I may fail to choose the words that let you know that I suffer. Or, perhaps, there may be something in you that keeps you from hearing or makes you turn away. More than a few experiences of acceptance are needed to cancel out the dread of rejection. In the one who is not living out of his or her own center, there springs up a driving urge to be attached to someone else's life. In that anxiety all kinds of thoughts are tended. What if I dare to speak and am not heard? I begin to picture myself lonelier than if I had kept my silence. In my mind's eye I see ancient wailing walls and envy those who, beating their fists upon those walls, find fellowship with other wailers.

How familiar are some of these fantasies, but they are nonetheless full of deceit. The person who gives them much attention will be dragged into the mire of self-pity. We do not make our confession for the sake of others or as a way to be received into their worlds. We make our confession for our own sakes and as a way to enter into our own worlds. When we begin to hear, through our opaque and clumsy words, what our own beings utter, then perhaps we can begin to hear what someone else is struggling to say. That is how communion begins.

In confession we learn something of the intensity of our feelings and discover things about ourselves we had not guessed. We are never diminished by our confession. Quite the opposite. We have the feeling of having expanded a little bit, and, actually, this is what happens. We come into possession of more of ourselves and so have more of ourselves to bring to a relationship. The shallow places of our lives begin to fill in. We see not only that we are sinned against, but that we sin. We are lifted into a wider world where we become aware of the wounds of others. We may even see a few places where our own knives cut. As we emerge from self-absorption, the process of belonging is begun.

Our fear ceases to be what it was. In tapping the resources of that inner Kingdom, we move closer to believing in love. It becomes clear that it is love which casts out fear. This is what Christianity is all about — becoming lovers. The mission of the Church is just loving people.

And our confession? *What is our confession? It is that we do not know how to love.* Until we have made that confession, there is nothing to be learned. We cannot even be a beginner with the beginners; and in the School of Christianity, there is nothing else to be but a beginner.

The alienation which grips so many today may reflect the loss of the ancient rite of confession. Those whose lives are most surrounded by people are often the ones who express inordinate hunger for community. We are slow to understand that the longing for a companion may reflect the inability to *be* a companion. We can pass through the world strangers to those for whom we were intended, failing to comprehend the gulf between us, much less desiring to bridge it. Or it may be that we are incapable of revealing ourselves in our humanness so that we can have the kind of conversation that fills up hollowness.

In *The New York Times Book Review* Edward Dahlberg wrote poignantly of lost opportunities for relationship when he reflected on his encounters with the esteemed novelist, Theodore Dreiser. He had longed to know Dreiser, but when he thought of getting in touch with the man, he pictured Dreiser engaged in the creation of another Titan. He wondered how he could possibly interrupt Dreiser. Besides, he imaged himself as a "raw prentice" with nothing of value to offer the great man. "Should I telephone him, he would surely hang up the receiver, and I would be mortally wounded." Finally Dahlberg took the "penultimate hazard." Dreiser asked him to come right to his apartment. Dahlberg later wrote these piercing lines describing the story of a relationship which he was uncertain he could call a friendship:

> My meetings with Dreiser continued, but I always was of the mind that I was ravaging his precious hours. Long after his death, I read that, at the time we became acquainted, his closest friend had died and he hoped that Edward Dahlberg might take the lost friend's place. What a glut of mulligrubs I had when I perused that single line in a biographical study of Dreiser. Time and again since then I have been bitten by the ever-hungry tooth of remorse. Good God, Theodore Dreiser needed me; and I, who have always been the beggar in any relationship, did not realize how desperately I required him.[1]

We read these lines and are somehow not the same. Dahlberg does what all artists do who are in touch with their feelings: he puts us in touch with our own feelings. Because the pain of his outcry is our own, we begin to see we can live in a gentler world where love is given and received. It is for this discovery that we make confession.

When remorse is real and not a whip, it has the possiblity of giving us a whole new attitude. Actually, confession is made for the revealing of our light — gifts of love, faith, and creativity. Understanding this, however, will not always make the resistance to confession less. If we exercise love, we become vulnerable. If we confess our gifts, we are apt to be asked to use them. *In the end, the sin we must all come to look at is the sin of withholding ourselves. This is the sin that keeps us beggars in life.* But how do we fully look at any sin without the help of confession? And, in the world today, confession is almost impossible.

THE REAL SELF

Sometimes we would like to think that confession is valued more highly in the church than in the secular world, but in reality, the situation in the church is not much different. Strange myths have grown up in Christendom about what it means to be a Christian. When we are baptized (or dedicated or saved or confirmed), we are stamped Christian, and henceforth we are in the mold of what a Christian should be. There is no place for us to go. We are supposed to be there already. Sermons, books, and classes keep outlining the marks of a Christian: a Christian is joyful, loving, fearless, the embodiment of the Sermon on the Mount and every other positive attribute. We either come to believe in our own perfection or we fall into despair over the contradictions in our lives and the life of the community.

Meanwhile, we keep debating the perplexing question as to why there sometimes seems to be more joy outside the church than in the church, and why many "non-Christians" are more loving and innovative than "Christians." We all know some disturbing people who disown the saving love of Christ and yet are more adventuresome and engaging than members of the church. So we continue the dreary discussions of how they got that way, until someone concludes that the Spirit of Christ is not limited to the church, but is also operative in those who are not "Christian." This explanation, which would hardly be acceptable to the nonbeliever, affords us noticeable relief. As long as this is why our innocent antagonists are doing as well as they are, we can go on believing in Christianity and waiting for their enlightenment.

The nagging problem of little fire in the church may persist, but when we have solved once more the huge dilemma of why "non-Christians" are more Christian than "Christians," we can afford to let the question of the sleeping church go until it is raised again. And it will be raised again. Spurious answers that evade the real issue leave us only temporarily convinced. Before long, in another context, with other people, we find ourselves embroiled in discussion of the same old questions.

The fact that we assume that all the "good" and "loving" people should be in the church is indicative of our misunderstanding of the nature of the church. We have even equated membership in the church with having arrived at a certain state of respectablity. We have no room for the maimed and outcast, thieves, adulterers, the wretched and tormented. No wonder we so often have an oppressive organization on our hands "full of dead men's bones and all uncleanness" (Matt. 23:27, RSV).

Confession cannot be found in a congregation that has taken the image of a saint or the description of the Kingdom person and made it the Christian ideal that "must" or "ought" to be lived out in the lives of its people. Our teachers and church leaders have done this more often than any of us who love the church would like to admit. In our own way we all do it. Bonhoeffer gave solemn warning to "the man who fashions a visionary ideal of community" and "demands that it be realized by God, by others, and by himself."[2] When an ideal becomes the dominant norm of what must be achieved by the members of a community, there are a variety of responses, all of which are destructive of "life together." Some people recognize that they cannot meet the expectations and, because they are not able to pretend, they despair of ever belonging. Others, who are perfectionists, increase their strivings, become themselves "keepers of the rules," and issue pronouncements of judgment.

A more common response is to conform to the ideal by repressing all the negative qualities in one's self. Many of us are lost in this way. We develop an unreal personality or what Jung has called a *persona*. We put on masks for others and finally come to believe in the masks ourselves, even to the point of taking pride in our false images.

Another common response to an "impossible ideal" is to withdraw altogether. Hundreds choose to leave the church and go in search of a community that will allow them to be fallible human beings on the pilgrimage of becoming whole. It is apt to be a futile search.

The whole spirit of confession is absent in most segments of our society. The young, the old, the blacks, the whites, the party in power, the reformers are never heard to make confession. The dominant note everywhere is self-righteousness. Humility is a quality peculiarly absent from today's life. People are not eager to confess that their programs might be less than adequate. They are intent upon advancing their own ideas and opinions. When this happens, there can be only violence. No unifying action goes on.

But it is not our concern that this happens in the world, which never claimed confession or knew it as a sacrament. Our concern is that confession has gone out of the church. The answer may be for the church to reject its glowing definitions of the "person in Christ."

Perhaps we should all agree that the Sermon on the Mount is not a text to take seriously. We could consider it simply as the ancient manual of a revolution that got off to a promising beginning, but was too extravagant and unrealistic in its claims. The "blessed" state of a person of the Kingdom is probably reached only in eternity and has nothing to do with the here-and-now of our lives. If we who are the church could arrive at this conclusion, we might be able to give up claiming to be what we are not. And this is our real need — an end to pretense. There is no salvation any other way. We must be ourselves.

For a fleeting moment it seems that the relinquishment of goals which are too lofty might be the solution. It may be drastic, but it frees us from having to live in the tension between what we are and what we "should" be. We can settle down and be our ordinary selves. Strange, though, how quickly the music goes out of what seems to be such a releasing and contemporary answer. Strange that it should give us a hollowness inside, as if, perhaps, it might not be good news at all.

Could it be that our real self is not so ordinary as we thought and that it takes a lot of struggle to discover that real self? We might have been deceived when we were led to think that "to do one's own thing" was easy. *Being true to one's self might even be what the whole gospel message is about.*

POSSIBILITIES

When we recover an inner stillness and go back to read again the Sermon on the Mount, nothing in us protests that it describes a level of being beyond our reach. In the silence of the soul where God's word is heard, we know the vision of the blessed person of the Kingdom to be authentic. The text comes down to us across the centuries precisely because it calls us to what is high in ourselves. And the text is not without witnesses. In every age they form a cloud around us. Every now and then, there appears in our company a person whose life awakens in us imagination, hope, mercy, qualities of courage and joy we did not know we possessed. We are given access to our possibilities.

A Bonhoeffer stripped of his clothing kneels naked to pray beneath the hangman's noose, and there stirs in us the thought that we, too, might have a relationship with the eternal that nothing can destroy.

One man's private act of prayer restores and sustains us.

Condemned as a traitor to the Third Reich, Father Alfred Delp, awaiting his Nazi executioners, lifts his fettered hands to bless his church and land, and mercy and forgiveness are nurtured in us.

Cesar Chavez goes to jail saying, "Although I think the judge is wrong, I'm not angry,"[3] and it becomes important to us to move beyond the place of our own anger. We are told the farm workers see in Cesar more than a leader. They want to be like him. They want to relate to other people as he does. In the presence of this man, migrant people, deprived of most of the benefits of our system, discover that they have a larger goal than better wages and medical funds. As important as these are, there is something more important. The life style of this man is the life style they want to make their own.

When we get right down to it, none of us wants to remain where we are. *We are not awake until there stirs in us the possibility of what we can become.* Then, and only then, can we begin a journey and belong to the migrant people of God. The absence, however, of models in all areas of our life has impoverished us. I have a friend who was afraid of old age because all the old people she knew were making life hard for themselves and hard for others. Unconsciously she had drawn up a blueprint of what old age is supposed to be and had thought that she was destined to live out that blueprint in her own life. Her torment vanished when a seventy-nine year old woman who communicated excitement and joy in life became her best friend.

Whether we are very young or middle-aged or old, we need those whose life styles speak to the yearning for pilgrimage that is written into our very nature. Herein lies the power of the Sermon on the Mount. It is a call to pilgrimage. No one is left without an example. This call to pilgrimage is made by One who embodies the life he describes. Our grievous error has been in taking the goals of the journey and using them as standards for everyone to "live up to." We have even used the Sermon as a description of the church, rather than as the call to which the church responds and the call which it issues. The text is not in error. The fault lies in our interpretation and use of it.

The text of the Sermon addresses us where we are. It tells us about a quality of life that is possible, but it is not deceived about our true condition. If we read past the beatitudes, we discover that the Sermon is addressed to us in our lostness. In line after line, the Sermon concerns itself with our disbelief and our fear. The Author knows how much we will do for approval and acceptance of others. He knows all about the dark ledgers in which we record the ways people misuse us or fail to appreciate us. The text assumes that we know very little about the importance of doing a thing simply for the joy of it. As for money, the Sermon reveals to us that this is where our security lies. The Speaker of the Sermon does not claim that things will change very fast. He is even careful to say that the way that leads to life is hard.

It is not the Sermon, after all, that we need to give up, but our understanding of the church as a people who have arrived at a certain place of joy or fearlessness or any other pinnacle. The church is simply a people who have glimpsed that Christ is Lord and are in the process of getting their houses off sand and onto rock. The church is a liberation movement. The people in it are the oppressed of the land who have awakened to the fact that they are not free.

If Christians have any distinguishing mark, it is that they have felt the trembling of their own foundations and raised the question of what they must do to be saved. Some have not even seen the sand on which they have built; others are in the anguish of that discovery; and others, while aware of it, have their houses full of "money changers" who are trying to drive some very reasonable bargains. It takes a long time to sweep the temple clean. There is a rather sweet sound to the drone of those familiar voices bickering over what the terms are and blaming others for not living up to them. In everyone's journey is a stage where one's attention is absorbed by the wickedness of the world. To come to the matter of one's own demon possession takes time. Without confession, it would be utterly impossible.

Central to the teaching of the early church was the admonition to "confess your sins to one another" (James 5:16, *RSV*). The fact that we no longer take this instruction seriously may account for the lack of fire or religious experience in the churches today.

SELF-EXAMINATION

When disciplines become disassociated from goals — and we keep the disciplines without understanding why, but simply because someone in authority has told us to do them — it is only a matter of time before we are weighted down by what was intended to help us move toward freedom. If we keep on after that, the oppression grows and grows until one day all of our dammed up feelings break loose, and we throw out the intolerable obligation to which we had so obediently submitted. After that, no one can mention authority or discipline or confession without triggering in us a composite of volatile emotions.

Our rebellion may be an important step in the discovery of our autonomy, but it does not assure our arriving at a mature detachment that will enable us to reexamine confession and discover what was real in this ancient sacrament of the church. Protestants have not practiced confession with any seriousness since the Reformation. The ironical fact is that the church described by Jesus was the confessing community, the community of sinners, the community where people could be themselves. Jesus was very much aware of the danger of becoming identified with ideal images.

He was speaking about our unconscious life when he told us in decisive terms that the one who is concerned with the speck in another's eye is a fraud. This is instruction in self-observation which is essential if we are to make real confession. As long as we attribute our discontent to circumstances or to the failure of others to respond as they "should," we are in trouble, and there is little possibility of our finding the community we long for. The pilgrimage Jesus talks about begins with looking to our own lives and finding there what blocks growth in our selves and, ultimately, blocks growth in others.

People engaged in self-examination will begin to make startling discoveries about themselves which, in confession, are brought into fuller consciousness. *We do not confess our faults in order that God may be better acquainted with them, but in order that the concreteness of words will increase our own understanding.* The psalmist said:

> Even before a word is on my tongue,
>   lo, O Lord, thou knowest it altogether.
>   — Psalm 139:4, *RSV*

Sometimes the situation is even more disturbing than the Scripture indicates. Not only does God know, but so does our sister or brother — a fact more difficult to bear. We all have shortcomings which, though completely hidden from us, are very obvious to our neighbors. This is an unsettling kind of information, if it is fully understood. We manage to avoid confrontation with it because the opposite is also true: no one can possibly know us as we are known to ourselves. This eclipses the fact that we can be ignorant of what others see in us.

We can be a long time in reaching the discovery that we have been following a self-defeating pattern all of our lives. At the same time, it can be information well known to our friends who have always been perplexed by it. Or we may say, "I can see how self-centered I have been." Those who know us sigh in relief because our discovery promises some change. But we are all blind to our own failings. We can even be ignorant of serious personality handicaps which give us pervasive feelings of unease. It may take long practice in self-observation to obtain any glimmering of understanding that our painful feelings are related to our choice of what Alfred Adler called a "mistaken lifestyle."

CHANGE

We are aware of how the hardened structures of society resist change, but those hardened structures that we externalize and call the enemy are really in ourselves. Within each of us there is something that wants to keep things as they are. Our whole self-identity is tied in with the present order. Is this not what Jesus was trying to tell us in the conversation with the man at the pool of Bethesda?

> Later on Jesus went up to Jerusalem for one of the Jewish festivals. Now at the Sheep-Pool in Jerusalem there is a place with five colonnades. Its name in the language of the Jews is Bethesda. In these colonnades there lay a crowd of sick people, blind, lame, and paralysed. Among them was a man who had been crippled for thirty-eight years. When Jesus saw him lying there and was aware that he had been ill a long time, he asked him, "Do you want to recover?" "Sir," he replied, "I have no one to put me in the pool when the water is disturbed, but while I am moving, someone else is in the pool before me." Jesus answered, "Rise to your feet, take up your bed and walk." The man recovered instantly, took up his stretcher, and began to walk.
>
> —John 5:1-9, *NEB*

Later in the story, Jesus finds the man in the temple and says to him, "Now that you are well again, leave your sinful ways, or you may suffer something worse." Here Jesus makes a direct connection between the man's sufferings and his problems. At some time it would be profitable to reflect on this connection, but now it is the startling question, "Do you want to recover?" that we need to consider as we make our confession. Do we really want to give up our illusions about life, our deceits about the kind of people we are, all those false images about the past and fantasies concerning the future? They may be our sins, in that they have kept us from living our lives fully, but they are comfortable and familiar, and in our internal establishment, they hold together our concept of who we are.

Take out even one little piece, and there is a trembling in the whole structure; such is the interconnectedness of all our inward workings. We cannot change in one little corner of our lives without feeling the reverberations in other corners. The question — "Do you want to recover?" — might even go to the root of things where the foundations would shake and the whole of us be in danger of collapse.

The man of the pool story made reply to the question by saying that he never had a chance. The cards were just stacked against him. "Poor me. I do not even have a friend. In the competition, I can't make it. I have not the advantages of others. But . . ." (There surely was a "but" to shore up self-esteem.) "But, I am patient. I am persevering. In adversity I wear a brave smile and am warmed by the thought that others see my plight and know me to be longsuffering."

Then did there come, in that conversation with Jesus, a time when the man gained enough detachment to take a penetrating look at himself? Was he able to make a few tentative movements toward responsibility, to ask himself some questions? "Why have I no friend to watch with me by this pool? What in me alienates people? Why do I erect walls between myself and others?" Or were his questions along another line: "What in me is satisfied with things as they are? Are there demands in life from which my disability protects me? How does my life style help me to manipulate others?"

Our chance to be healed comes when the waters of our own life are disturbed. We can plunge into them and emerge new, or we can sit there by the churning depths of our inner world, justifying our existence as it is. We know that the man by the pool could not, by himself, save himself. He needed someone to ask the question that would enable him to confess his secret griefs. Can members of the body of Christ enter into relationship with each other in a way that offers the gift of confession?

Never think that change is easy or that it comes suddenly or without pain. That is a storybook world. We are each the one to whom the question is addressed: "Do you want to recover?" We are each the man by the well. We are each "The Prisoner of Chillon":

> It was at length the same to me
> Fettered or fetterless to be,
>   I learned to love despair.
> And thus when they appeared at last,
> And all my bonds aside were cast,
> These heavy walls to me had grown
> A hermitage — and all my own!
> And half I felt as they were come
> To tear me from a second home:
> - - - - - -
> My very chains and I grew friends,
> So much a long communion tends
> To make us what we are: — even I
> Regained my freedom with a sigh.
>   — George Gordon, Lord Byron
>   "The Prisoner of Chillon"

It is a strange and frightening discovery to find that the sacrificial life that Jesus is talking about is the giving up of our chains—to discover that what binds us is also what gives us comfort and a measure of feeling safe. Change, while it has promise, will take from us something we have found sweet. The image we have of ourselves may keep us from wholeness, but it has some very satisfying compensations. There are dividends in being known as the one for whom nothing ever works out. It is never easy to lose the paradise of one's innocence and to have to struggle with growing up and being held accountable for one's own life. There are all kinds of anxieties in having to leave the land one knows and to be on one's way toward a strange land. No wonder Jesus comments so often on the people who look and look, but see nothing; and hear and hear, but do not understand. If we really saw and really heard, we might turn to him and become involved with a migrant people who may have no place to lay their heads when night comes.

Not only does change threaten something deep in us and call into being all kinds of resistance, it also threatens our friends. They, too, prefer the status quo. They may find us difficult to put up with at times, but something in them is also threatened at the prospect of any real change in us. They would be glad to have us give up a few irritating habits, provided we stay essentially as we are.

Not only do we resist change in ourselves, but we resist change in others. We wonder whether the changing person will still belong to us in the same way. Will that person exercise a power that will evoke envy and jealousy in us? Will that person support our little plans and projects in the same way? Only when we ourselves are changing persons does some of the threat go out of these questions.

Does it seem to you that the discussion has wandered from confession to change? This could not be avoided. Confession leads to change, just as self-observation leads to confession. In fact, if we were to work in depth with any aspect of our lives, we would discern its close connection with everything else in us. We would be able to see the interrelatedness of all the facets of our being, and to understand how change in one part of us is communicated to all the other parts.

One of the hidden reasons why we avoid the practice of confession may be so that we do not have to change. The paradox, however, is that the change we fear is also the change we want. We would like to keep our story secret, but we also yearn to share it.

An attraction of the many small support groups meeting today is the opportunity they offer to participants to tell their stories—to bring to speech unshared pain. The leader of one small group I know always begins her sessions with a simple statement that says in essence, "I see you. I recognize that you have needs as a person and that you are entitled to what you think and feel. If you tell me your feelings, thoughts and needs, I will listen and will not run away." Those words are especially welcomed when we are troubled by feelings and thoughts and needs that do not seem very acceptable. They are words that invite us to struggle with the obstacles that stand in the way of saying who we are.

CONFRONTATION

The general confessions in the litanies of worship were never intended to take the place of individual confession. They do not directly reflect the disturbing issues of our private lives. No one comes forward out of the congregation to address to us the question that enables us to confront ourselves as we are. Unrecognized guilt piles on guilt until we begin responding in destructive ways. It cannot be otherwise. *We each need someone who will ask us to give an account of ourselves, so that we can face into our lives and can confess who we really are.* Surely John felt confirmation at another level of being and a heightened sense of destiny when he made reply to the questions addressed to him:

> This is the testimony which John gave when the Jews of Jerusalem sent a deputation of priests and Levites to ask him who he was. He confessed without reserve and avowed, "I am not the Messiah." "What then? Are you Elijah?" "No," he replied. "Are you the prophet we await?" He answered "No." "Then who are you?" they asked. "We must give an answer to those who sent us. What account do you give of yourself?" He answered in the words of the prophet Isaiah: "I am a voice crying aloud in the wilderness, 'Make the Lord's highway straight.' "
>
> —John 1:19-23, *NEB*

COMMUNITY

Perhaps, in the small group movement of the churches where persons feel enough acceptance to share their real feelings, the church will recover again the grace of confession. The danger here is that, in an effort to avoid a moralistic kind of judgment, we might go to the opposite pole and give to each other an easy kind of comfort.

When we begin to be in earnest about the Christian faith, we can see how some of the practices of the church, originally introduced to give encouragement and support, have been discarded because of misuse. Penance was such a practice. People making confession were given penance appropriate to the transgression so that they would be halted long enough to consider the seriousness of any action or attitude that disrupted their relationship with self and God and others; the penance would also lodge in their consciousness something to draw on if the temptation should arise again.

So often our confession has no healing effect because we are unaware of what our real problems are. In today's world there are probably as many who will identify with darkness in themselves as those who will identify with an idealized image. Some people experience themselves as "not all right" and willingly confess to any sin that is mentioned. It is understandable that this neurotic use of confession has had a part in the rejection of the practice.

In a community that has a life in depth, the misuse of confession is greatly reduced, simply because the on-going life of the group offers opportunity for real engagement with others and with self. Members are together at times of fatigue and anxiety when weaknesses become apparent. In such a situation the truly confessing community is apt to emerge. The members have the opportunity to experience each other under a variety of circumstances. They know what it is to hurt one another and to stand in need of forgiveness.

One of the paradoxes of life is that our very strengths, under conditions of stress, often become our weaknesses. When we share the common life of a group, we are polished by the friction of our rough edges rubbing together. Jealousy, envy, and rivalry are all part of the picture. The seven deadly sins are not old-fashioned to communities trying to forge a style of life that will make a corporate witness. Any life lived with others in depth will bring to the surface negative responses. This is one of the painful realities of life in community.

For a community to exist in any way that matters, its members must deal with those feelings which prevent their moving toward unity. Every member must mediate acceptance to every other member, despite any transgression, or the group will find itself limping along without any real power. When even one member of a group rejects one other member, the corporate strength of the group is diminished. This may be why our groups so often lack inner vitality. And yet acceptance of another sometimes comes only through a painful kind of confrontation when, with inner trembling, we dare to confess what we are feeling. This is different from "telling another off" or withdrawing into silence, both of which are violent acts and, like all violence, call forth outrage in the other.

Authentic confession is never easy. It requires courage; and it is seldom accomplished unless all the members of the group are committed to growing in consciousness, and unless the dialogue has as its end the deepening of relationships. We seek not to change others by our confession, but to change the disturbing feelings in ourselves.

Without confession, we will find it difficult—if not impossible—to be a people together on a journey. We cannot be in community with others without the emergence of our shadow selves. This development is not to be deplored, for it is one of the very reasons why we must have community. We do not know what we have to overcome in ourselves until we are up against those whose needs, opinions, and life styles clash with our own needs, opinions, and life styles. As long as we are sheltered from the give-and-take of a wide variety of relationships, we can maintain illusions of how "nice" we are. Then we will never be confronted with that in ourselves which we must overcome to take the next step in our pilgrimage. In a sense we will be left without an inner goal. Gradually, without our even being aware of it, the meaning will go out of life. Any time we consider our inner work done, we go into retirement. A gloom settles over us. The death that Scripture so often talks about describes such an inner state. Finally, the decay, imperceptible as it is, will begin to show in the rigidity of our bearing. The hardening of life forces will be reflected in our attitudes and reactions to events around us.

In his book *Shantung Compound,* Langdon Gilkey[4] tells the story of two years that he spent in a Japanese internment camp during World War II. The camp was an enforced community, but it nonetheless illustrates how difficult it is to work out a satisfactory covenant even when our very survival is dependent on it. Compared with other internment camps, this one was not too bad. There was no cruelty, but there was a lack of space, never enough food, and always the threat that the meager provisions might cease altogether. Under these extraordinary pressures, the most pious missionaries proved selfish. They acted in ways that, under ordinary circumstances, they probably would have thought impossible. Gilkey does not tell whether they looked back on the experience and came to a better understanding of their own frailty. In a truly confessing community there would have been opportunity to reflect on their responses and learn from them, and thus to be people on the journey of becoming whole.

We talk a lot today about the mission of the church, which is essential if the church is to take its servant role in society and position itself with the wretched of the earth. But we also need that mission for our own growth. If we are to know ourselves, we must be up against each other at places of stress when things are not going well. We can all say how we think we would behave under certain circumstances, but few of us know ourselves well enough to be sure. We cry with Peter that we will be loyal to the end—loyal to our convictions, loyal to our friends, loyal to our God. Unless we make a concentrated effort, however, or unless life jolts us out of our complacency with a Shantung Compound kind of experience, we are in grave danger of not knowing what our confession should be.

In the give-and-take of life in community, there will be times when we feel crowded and stepped on. We will feel that we lack space in our lives, just as they lacked space in the Shantung Compound. For this reason, in the small group, confession is being rediscovered as an authentic agent of God's healing, without which the group cannot deal with its problems and move on. Despite our thinking that confession must be made in a familiar "church" context if we are to be in touch with the supernatural, it is confession in the liturgical form that has lost meaning. Perhaps that meaning can be restored in conversation which is carried on with awareness that *the one who speaks confesses and those who listen are priests.*

It is, of course, possible for us to share ourselves in such a way that the confessional nature of our conversation is not evident. This can be a way of unburdening without having to come to grips with judgment. Ordinary conversations like this go on all the time. Even though the sacramental dimension of confession is absent from most therapy groups, it is still interesting to note that the members of these groups agree not to reveal to others what is talked about by members— an agreement comparable to the charge of secrecy given to the priest who hears confession. The difference in these situations is that no absolution is pronounced, and there is no conscious seeking of a relationship with Jesus Christ as well as with the members of one's community.

The Christian community, if it is to experiment with new forms of confession, must be more self-conscious in its quest and state again that to sin means to "miss the mark," and that the mark is the Kingdom of God. After that, all the other current definitions of sin— the failure to use one's gifts, or to realize one's potential, or to live one's own life fully—can be added as clarifying statements of what keeps us from the ultimate goal of the high call of God in Christ. By themselves, these definitions of sin are quite satisfactory for those outside the church, but the church is a people who claim citizenship in two cities—the city of human beings and the City of God. It is a people who believe that there is a power available to those who gather in the name of Christ and who listen and serve in his name. It is to this supernatural power that we want to open ourselves as we confess to one another who we are.

At first the account that we give of ourselves may be faltering and superficial, but it is movement toward seeing ourselves as we are and taking the next step in the awakening process. We do not have to be where we are not, or force ourselves, or let others push us into giving accounts that we are not ready to give.

SECRETS

Community will not exist unless we can learn to share our lives, but neither will there be any community where there is not a deep respect for privacy. One of the brighter discoveries of growing up is that one does not have to lie to keep a secret. There are questions addressed to us that we do not have to answer. We each have parts of our soul that need bear the prints of only our own footsteps.

But if there are secrets that we can safely keep from others, *there are no secrets that we can safely keep from ourselves*. Scripture says, "Take no part in the unfruitful works of darkness, but instead expose them . . . for anything that becomes visible is light" (Eph. 5:11,13, *RSV*). But very few of us will be able to uncover our hidden faults unless we struggle to put into words for another the secrets of which we are aware. As we struggle to put our feeling into words, new understanding breaks.

This does not mean that to have a flashing insight about one's self and to be able to say to another, "This is who I am," is to be assured of change. Change is always precious, comes slowly, and has a high cost. It can give the appearance of having occurred at one breathless juncture, but on the way to every peak moment are plateau stretches where it will seem to us that we work without any return for our labor. Those stretches make possible the specific occasions we can pinpoint as places of change. Our "instant-demanding" age has discovered no "instant" way to be reborn, though it runs after and indiscriminately embraces anything that promises such a way. The foundations of the change that seem sudden have been well laid and carefully built upon.

MEDITATION

An insight is a glimpse of truth and therefore of utmost importance; but if it is to introduce change in us, we must stay awake and guard it from being choked out by lies. Christ said, in one of his parables about the Kingdom of Heaven, that "while men were sleeping, his enemy came and sowed weeds among the wheat and went away" (Matt. 13:25, *RSV*). It is easy to lose in unconscious states one's tenuous hold on truth, to let the patterns of a lifetime that kept truth from view crowd in again. If I say to my sister or brother in Christ, "This is who I am," the truth has been externalized and made easier to grasp at another level of understanding; but it still has to be tended, lest it be like the corn that has no root and withers under the heat of the sun. *For truth to be deep in us, we need to meditate upon it.*

I heard a story which stays with me and continues to instruct. The central figure was an educated and cultured gentleman. One evening he stayed with two colleagues at his laboratory to work on a project they were all anxious to complete. When they had finished late that night, he invited them to his home for coffee. The conversation moved from their work at the lab to art, and he fell to sharing with them his interest in Greek architecture. Remembering a new volume that he had on the subject, he took it down from the shelf and handed it to his more advantaged co-worker, who quickly glanced at the pages and returned it to him. He was already putting the book back on the shelf when he glimpsed from the corner of his eye the hand of the other man extended to receive the book. The picture hardly registered. He did not come to terms with what had happened until later when he was in bed, and then he saw again the hand of the other man reaching to receive the book he had never offered. Unconsciously he had made the judgment that this man, being self-tutored, would not be interested in art. In an automatic way he had excluded him.

The "considerate" host had not thought himself capable of treating another fellow human like this, but he had enough understanding to know that this was not an isolated incident in his life. He knew he had glimpsed something in himself of which he was only dimly aware. He left his bed and spent the rest of the night sitting in his study reflecting on what had happened. He wanted the picture of it burned in his mind and heart so that it would keep him alert and help him avoid the possibility of his going through life ignoring the outstretched hands of his friends. Martin Buber defines sin as our failure to grant to others their pleas for community. Certainly this was the sin that was dealt with that long night.

The story is a poignant one in itself, but it also contains important help on how to hang on to and protect those scraps of self-knowledge that come to us all. So often the resolve to do better meets with consistent failure. The outcome is discouragement. We despair that we can ever be different, and we grow in dislike of ourselves. Actually, our broken resolves offer material germane to meditation. When we are consistent in observing ourselves, what we very early discover is that, given the same stimuli, we can be counted on to respond over and over again in the the same way. At least, in this one respect, no one is very complex. Instead of deploring our reactions, we need to reflect deeply on them and on those situations that evoke them. It is also well to remember that they do not represent the whole of us.

The result of this pondering will be a gaining of distance from the part of us that acts in such an unsatisfactory manner. Being less identified with negative behavior, we can be more accepting of it. Acceptance leads to understanding, and understanding leads to change. Meditation on our responses to persons and events can be a powerful tool in our striving to be free persons. When combined with confession, it adds greatly to the possibility of our growing in consciousness. We might begin the practice of meditation by learning to hold before us each night a fragment of our day, looking at it without judgment, turning it this way and that way, until our understanding of it deepens, and we can see and hear and turn to be healed.

A good book to have on one's shelf, if only to read from time to time its confirming title, is *I'm OK—You're OK* by Thomas A. Harris. The book itself has an equally helpful message. In the early pages Dr. Harris cites the work of Dr. Wilder Penfield, a neurosurgeon from McGill University in Montreal. During brain surgery on patients with focal epilepsy, Penfield conducted experiments in which he "touched the temporal cortex of the brain of the patient with a weak electric current transmitted through a galvanic probe."[5] The patient was always conscious and able to talk to the doctor. When the brain's memory cortex was touched by the electric probe, past experiences and feelings were relived by the patient and reported to the neurosurgeon as though they were indeed taking place all over again. Harris reports that Penfield's long research on many patients gives evidence that the brain, which has recorded in detail and stored up everything that has been in our conscious awareness, is capable of playing back the past in the present. "The brain functions as a high fidelity tape recorder."[6]

One of the important conclusions Harris draws from Penfield's work is that "recollections are evoked by the stimuli of day-to-day experience in much the same way that they are evoked artificially by Penfield's probe."[7] Something occurs in the present and touches off an old event and the feeling that accompanied it, so that we respond to the present out of the past. If we have enough experience of "space," we will be able to stand off and observe ourselves and note when our behavior is inappropriate, or when the situation does not warrant the intensity of our response. Penfield's experiments give us an idea of what we are up against in trying to effect change in ourselves, even when we see what needs to be changed. The problem is not all psychological or spiritual, as we may have thought. These studies indicate that our responses have a biological structure.

Meditation and confession are ways of firmly establishing in consciousness, and thus in the storehouse of the brain, other facts that will help the new in us do battle with the old. Often we try to change something in ourselves by violent combat with it. Even when we are successful, keeping vigil over the vanquished enemy requires all kinds of energy. We dare not expose ourselves to anything which might threaten the position we have obtained by much sacrifice. Our attitude toward life becomes unyielding and defensive, so uneasy is the peace that we have made within, and so uncertain are we as to when we might have to make war again.

The change which comes through understanding, however, is of a different nature. The practice of meditation can give us a feeling of separation from what we are observing in ourselves. The gate is then opened for the comprehending that transforms feelings, or that takes them and returns them to us as manageable forces. Even the "evil urge" in us that we acknowledge and call by name is deprived, by the act of observing, of its power to control our life and destiny.

While all things are subjects for our pondering, there are times when our confession is best made after meditation on Scripture. There is the life style that judges our own life style. There is articulated over and over again the vocation to which our deeper selves make response. Without meditation on Scripture, we will not know the change which reaches to the center of our being. There will be no real discovery of self. Any change we do experience will be on a very ordinary level of existence and will tend to become self-serving. Meditation will then lose the possibility of putting us in touch with what is higher in ourselves.

When we meditate on Scripture, we move into the presence of the One who said, "I AM that I AM." We grow aware that we, made in the image of God, have these words also hidden some place in ourselves, and that in confession we draw closer to our own *I am-ness*. We still see the suffering that we cannot explain, but we become aware of how little it is compared with the suffering that is in the world because of fear. It is given to us to know that life can be lived on an entirely different level, and we wonder if we can attain to it.

> And I said: "Woe is me! For I am lost;
> for I am a man of unclean lips;
> and I dwell in the midst of a people
> of unclean lips . . ."
> —Isaiah 6:5, *RSV*

TRANSFORMATION

But there is more than this insight of how things are with us. There comes, in its time, the assurance that our life situation can be utterly different. We begin to understand the meaning of transformation because it is happening to us. A friend said it this way:

> "I despaired because my life was in pieces, but I read that Book, and I read it, and read it, and I felt all together again, only I thought of myself as a cracked pot that had been pasted together. I thought I would always be like that, but then one day that image changed, too. I knew I wasn't an old cracked pot any longer. I was a beautiful Ming vase."

Those words describe transformation better than the words of a poet. We read Scripture and make our confession, and read Scripture and make our confession, and then one day something happens. We begin to see that we hold in our hands a Book that is a manual for change. No ordinary Book is this. It is concerned with a revolution of consciousness. It is not only talking of the new being, it is giving instructions for *becoming* the new being. Any earnest following of those instructions makes it abundantly clear that, while everything is asked of us and we must do everything, the very change that we see and yearn for and cannot live without is not in our power to effect. *While we must do everything, there is nothing that we can do. Something has to come from beyond us.* There then remains but one thing to do: to take our confession on our lips and throw ourselves upon the mercy of our Lord. Perhaps then waters will flow around us and we will hear a voice saying, "With thee I am well pleased."

John proclaimed a baptism in token of repentance, for the forgiveness of sins, and Jesus came to be baptized. Afterward, Jesus said to someone who listened and wrote it down, "I heard a voice from heaven say, 'Thou art my beloved Son; with thee I am well pleased' " (Luke 3:22, *RSV*). Only then did Jesus begin his ministry of preaching the good news.

When we, too, hear that voice, we shall kneel to make the confession toward which all confessions lead: Jesus is Lord. We shall no longer need a book that has a confirming title. That title will be written upon our hearts and there will be nothing that can keep us from preaching in towns and cities, "You're OK, I'm OK."

If one of us should then be asked, "Who gave you authority to tell me that my sins are forgiven," the answer can be, "I AM sent me."

EXERCISE 1:

Acknowledging and Accepting Your Dark Side

This first exercise is to help you become more conscious of those qualities in yourself that you would not like another to discover. As you meditate and become more aware of these "dark" qualities, keep a list of them in a journal or notebook. Become acquainted with your response to the negative parts of yourself. Do you treat those qualities with contempt? Do you speak disparagingly of yourself, e.g., "That was a stupid thing to do," or "How can I be so clumsy?" After confessing your faults, do you go on to condemn yourself for them?

The purpose of this first group of writings is not only to help you become more aware of your shadow self, but also, in the name of Jesus Christ, to accept the unacceptable in yourself — to love the enemy of your peace, even when that enemy is a member of your own household. Listen to what this dark side of you has to say. Try to understand its complaints and ill behavior — why it carries on the way it does, causing you all kinds of unease. This negative self may have an important message for you. Listen, and try to discover what it is. Every feeling serves a purpose. If you feel guilty when things are going well for you, live into that feeling. When did you first have it? If the feeling does not seem related to anything in the present, it may have origins in some past experience. Use the readings to help you in your self-examination.

Remember that you are a co-creator with God and, whereas you must struggle for your own salvation, you do not do it alone. You cannot by yourself save yourself from that which keeps you from realizing your potential to love. In Christ we find that the human and the divine complete each other. In our confession Christ draws close, for he did not come for the righteous, but for sinners.

Each night look back over your day and confess your sins to the One who can help you out of the webs in which you are entangled and trapped. If you feel safe enough, confess your problems to another person whom you can trust to listen in the name of Christ. The final word is never sin; it is always redemption.

UNDERSTANDING YOURSELF

Jesus said,
If those trying to entice you say to you, "Look, the kingdom is
   in heaven," then the birds will have an advantage over you.
If they say to you, "Look, it is in the sea," then the fish will
   have an advantage over you.
But the kingdom is inside you and outside of you. When you
   really understand yourselves, then you will be understood
   and you will know that you are the sons of the Living Father.
But if you do not understand yourselves, you will be in poverty
   and you will be poverty.

The Gospel According to Thomas,
Logion 3

LOVING AND BEING LOVED

I once knew a very old married couple who radiated a tremendous happiness. The wife especially, who was almost unable to
move because of old age and illness and in whose kind old face
the joys and sufferings of many years had etched a hundred
runes, was filled with such gratitude for life that I was touched to
the quick. Involuntarily I asked myself what could possibly be
the source of this kindly old person's radiance. Otherwise they
were very common people and their room indicated only the
most modest comfort. But suddenly I knew where it all came
from, for I saw these two speaking to each other and their eyes
hanging upon each other. All at once it became clear to me that
this woman was dearly loved. And it was as if she were like a
stone that has been lying in the sun for years and years, absorbing
all its radiant warmth, and now was reflecting back cheerfulness
and warmth and serenity.

Let me express it this way. It was not because she was this kind
of cheerful and pleasant person that she was loved by her husband all those years. It was probably the other way around.
Because she was so loved, she became the person I now saw
before me.

This thought continued to pursue me and the more it pursued me, the more it lost all its merely edifying and sentimental features, until finally they were gone altogether. For if this is true, then I surely must come to the following conclusion. If my life partner or my friend or just people generally often seem to be so strange and I ask myself: "Have I made the right marriage, the right friendship; is this particular person really the one who is suited to me?" — then I cannot answer this question in the style of a neutral diagnosis which would list the reasons for and against. For what happens then is that the question turns back upon myself, and then it reads: "Have I perhaps bestowed too little love upon this other person, that he has become so cold and empty? Have I perhaps caused him to become what perhaps he really has become? The other person, whom God has joined to me, is never what he is apart from me. *He is not only bone of my bone; he is also boredom of my boredom and lovelessness of my lovelessness.*"

And it is exactly the same with our relation to God. If a person is steeped in emptiness and boredom and is tired of life, the reason for it is that he has not allowed himself to be loved by God and has not put himself in his hands. One who does not love makes the other person wither and dry up. And one who does not allow himself to be loved dries up too. For love is a creative thing.

> Helmut Thielicke
> *How the World Began*
> (pp. 99-100)

SECURITY

In the process of reaching maturity and autonomy most of us do strive for security by trying to organize the universe around ourselves. And most of us learn only through the suffering and estrangement which attend egocentricity that this way leads not to security, but to an endlessly precarious and ultimately fruit-

less attempt to twist reality into meeting our private specifi-
cations . . .

We reach our highest freedom not by asserting our own interests
against the world, but by devoting ourselves in fellowship to a
way of life which reaches personal fulfillment along with, and
partly *through,* the fulfillment of others. We reach security only
by a trustful acceptance of the full truth about ourselves and
others, not by evasion of it. Healing power is latent in men
because it is latent "in the nature of things." Hence it is not surprising that men and women have found in Christ the supreme
disclosure of what coincidence between human beatitude and
divine love means. Christ is Saviour as He opens, for each man,
the way whereby that individual can move toward such coincidence. This involves moving forward into a deepened recognition of failure, impotence and need at many points. But the divine
forgiveness which He discloses always has been and always will
be accessible to men. We experience divine forgiveness as that
"making right" of our lives which occurs when we turn away
from fighting ourselves, and others, and the truth itself, and turn
trustfully toward the divine power which surrounds us and can
work through us. This experience of reconciliation, despite past
failures and unsolved problems in the present, makes men actually
more lovable, more discerning, more capable of devoting themselves to goods which enrich all humanity.

> David E. Roberts
> *Psychotherapy and a Christian
> View of Man* (pp. 134-135)

SELF-DECEPTION

If we claim to be sinless, we are self-deceived and strangers to
the truth. If we confess our sins, he is just, and may be trusted to
forgive our sins and cleanse us from every kind of wrong; but if
we say we have committed no sin, we make him out to be a liar,
and then his word has no place in us.

> I John 1:8-10, *NEB*

KNOWING YOURSELF

The all-knowing One does not get to know something about the maker of the confession, rather the maker of confession gets to know about himself. Therefore, do not raise the objections against the confession that there is no point in confiding to the all-knowing One that which He already knows. Reply first to the question whether it is not conferring a benefit when a man gets to know something about himself which he did not know before. A hasty explanation could assert that to pray is a useless act, because a man's prayer does not alter the unalterable. But would this be desirable in the long run? Could not fickle man easily come to regret that he had gotten God changed? The true explanation is therefore at the same time the one most to be desired. The prayer does not change God, but it changes the one who offers it. It is the same with the substance of what is spoken. Not God, but you, the maker of the confession, get to know something by your act of confession.

Søren Kierkegaard
Purity of Heart (pp. 50-51)

FORGIVING YOURSELF

If guilt is to be healed, the victim must be reconciled to himself. Were his feelings mainly outgoing, there would be little problem: if he felt nothing but grief at the damage which he had caused to others, reconciliation with them would follow easily. He would have no hesitation in saying "I am sorry." But because his feelings are usually complicated by inner remorse and self-rejection, reconciliation becomes difficult, sometimes even impossible, to achieve. The forgiveness which others would give him is blocked by his inability to forgive himself. Therefore the problem of guilt is nothing other than one facet of the problem of self-hatred.

Malcolm France
The Paradox of Guilt (pp. 19-20)

GOING ON

I think God must be very old and very tired. Maybe he used to look splendid and fine in his general's uniform, but no more. He's been on the march a long time, you know. And look at his rag-tag little army! All he has for soldiers are you and me. Dumb little army. Listen! The drum beat isn't even regular. Everyone is out of step. And there! You see? God keeps stopping along the way to pick up one of his tinier soldiers who decided to wander off and play with a frog, or run in a field, or whose foot got tangled in the underbrush. He'll never get anywhere that way. And yet, the march goes on.

Do you see how the marchers have broken up into little groups? Look at that group up near the front. Now, there's a snappy outfit. They all look pretty much alike — at least they're in step with each other. That's something! Only they're not wearing their shoes. They're carrying them in their hands. Silly little band. They won't get far before God will have to stop again.

Or how about that other group over there? They're all holding hands as they march. The only trouble with this is the men on each end of the line. Pretty soon they realize that one of their hands isn't holding onto anything — one hand is reaching, empty, alone. And so they hold hands with each other, and everybody marches around in circles. The more people holding hands, the bigger the circle. And, of course, a bigger circle is deceptive because as we march along it looks like we're going someplace, but we're not. And so God must stop again. You see what I mean? He'll never get anywhere that way!

If God were more sensible he'd take his little army and shape them up. Why, whoever heard of a soldier stopping to romp in a field? It's ridiculous. But even more absurd is a general who will stop the march of eternity to go and bring him back. But that's God for you. His is no endless, empty marching. He is going somewhere. His steps are deliberate and purposive. He may be old, and he may be tired. But he knows where he's going. And he means to take every last one of his soldiers with him. Only there aren't going to be any forced marches. And, after all, there are frogs and flowers, and thorns and underbrush along the way. And even though our foreheads have been signed with the sign of the cross, we are only human. And most of us are afraid and lonely and would like to hold hands or cry or run away. And we don't know where we are going, and we can't seem to trust God — especially when it's dark out and we can't see him! And he won't go on without us. And that's why it's taking so long.

Listen! The drum beat isn't even regular. Everyone is out of step. And there! You see? God keeps stopping along the way to pick up one of his tinier soldiers who decided to wander off and play with a frog, or run in a field, or whose foot got tangled in the underbrush. He'll never get anywhere that way!

And yet, the march goes on . . .

> Martin Bell
> *The Way of the Wolf* (pp. 91-93)

KNOWING YOU ARE LOVED

My children, mark me, I pray you. Know! God loves my soul so much that his very life and being depend upon his loving me whether he would or not. To stop God loving me would be to rob him of his Godhood.

> Meister Eckhart
> *Meister Eckhart* (p. 26)

KEEPING AWARE

The primary purpose of confession is to keep people aware of their true condition, of the tension between the good and evil in themselves. "If we say we have no sin, we deceive ourselves, and the truth is not in us" (I John 1:8). "Therefore confess your sins to one another, and pray for one another, that you may be healed" (James 5:16). The most dangerous thing that can happen to us is that we become unaware of, or unconscious of, our sin and guilt. If there is to be growth of soul, such conflicts must not be pushed under so far that we lose track of them. If the church would make the individual man aware of evil, the evil that is lurking behind every good, and bring him to a recognition of the sin and guilt within his own soul and of the tremendous part which confession and forgiveness play in achieving wholeness, confession, both formal and informal, must necessarily find a primary place in her life. Such conflicts, trials, and sins, by being held consciously before us, can ultimately be resolved and bring healing to the soul. But, on the other hand, the tension of holding this in consciousness is often more than the soul can endure, so it must commit itself and its sin to God to whom the ultimate solution is known, and from whom the forgiveness and healing come.

Charles B. Hanna
Face of the Deep (pp. 95-96)

KEEPING WATCHFUL

Watch and pray
   that you may not enter into temptation;
the spirit indeed is willing,
but the flesh is weak.

Matthew 26:41, *RSV*

HIDDEN FAULTS

Who can discern his errors?
   Clear thou me from hidden faults.
Keep back thy servant also from presumptuous sins;
   let them not have dominion over me!
Then I shall be blameless,
   and innocent of great transgression.

Psalm 19:12-13, *RSV*

INNER KNOWLEDGE

Search me, O God, and know my heart!
Try me and know my thoughts!
And see if there be any wicked way in me,
and lead me in the way everlasting!

Psalm 139: 23-24, *RSV*

INNER SEARCH

The heart is deceitful above all things,
    and desperately corrupt;
    who can understand it?
"I the Lord search the mind
    and try the heart,
to give to every man according to his ways,
    according to the fruit of his doings."

Jeremiah 17:9-10, *RSV*

SECRETS

Wrong secrets and those kept wrongly cut one off and act like poison from within, so that confession is cathartic and communication therapeutic. The paranoid demand for absolute loyalty, that fear of betrayal and exposure, shows that one is no longer able to love and be hurt. Loving goes where betrayal is possible, otherwise there is no risk. Loving in safety is the smaller part of loving. Secrecy of this sort is a defence leading to paranoid loneliness: alone with one's secrets and no one to trust. Another secret kept wrongly is that of the small child who clutches his secret in powerful exercise of omnipotence. For him it is necessary, but the grown-up child goes on in this pattern, dominating by holding back. Both paranoid and childish secrecy keep one wrongly apart.

To keep a secret means etymologically to keep something apart, separate. Secrecy is basic for individuality. In a family, for instance, no individual personalities can develop unless the members keep some secrets *with* one another and other secrets *from* one another. What you keep secret keeps you apart, and in your secret life you begin to discover your individual soul. (One reason why it is so difficult to keep secrets is just because it is so hard to maintain one's individuality.)

By telling a secret one lets another into the sacred preserve of one's individuality. One keeps one's secrets until one feels that the other person with whom one is about to share a secret also views it as sacred. For this, trust must be built up between two people.

James Hillman
Suicide and the Soul (p. 173)

DECEIVING YOURSELF

Confession, as we know, can also be used for self-deception. The more intelligent and cultured a man is, the more subtly he can humbug himself. No moderately intelligent person should believe himself either a saint or a sinner. Both would be a conscious lie. Rather he should keep shamefacedly silent about his moral qualities, ever mindful of his abysmal sinfulness on the one hand, and of his meritoriously humble insight into this desolate state of affairs on the other. All that the younger Blumhardt remarked to an acquaintance of mine, on his making an agonizingly contrite confession of sin, was: "Do you think God is interested in your miserable muck?" Blumhardt had evidently noted the trick that makes drawing-room confession so attractive.

C.G. Jung
The Development of Personality,
vol. 17, Collected Works (p. 79)

HIDING YOUR DARK SIDE

We cannot stand the sight of our dark side, so we repress it, push it under, thinking we have thereby disposed of it. But we have not. We have simply pushed it into a place where it both has us in its grip and automatically projects itself on the person or the nation we do not like; so the tension we will not stand in ourselves is carelessly and irresponsibly cast out to increase the tension and strife and anguish of our world . . . Jung saw it as a psychological law that what we will not suffer inwardly through conscious recognition of our shadow, we will suffer outwardly as the result of our unconscious projections into the world around us. He thereby gives Christians the most awesome charge that they can possibly receive throughout their lives: the withdrawal of their projections upon others, and dealing with their shadow themselves. Here one almost senses the dimension of the "hellfire and brimstone" preaching, once so characteristic of the church's message. Has it faded out of church evangelism only to rise anew in the awesome heights and depths of the new psychology?

Charles B. Hanna
The Face of the Deep (pp. 100- 101)

POSSIBILITY OF FORGIVENESS

By speaking about articulation as a form of leadership we have already suggested the place where the future leader will stand. Not up-there, out-there, far-away or secretly hidden, but in the midst of his people with an utmost visibility.

If we now realize that the future generation is not only an inward generation asking for articulation but also a fatherless generation looking for a new kind of authority, we have then to ask what the nature of this authority will be. I cannot find a better word than *compassion*. It is compassion that has to become the core and even the nature of authority. When the Christian leader wants to consider himself a man of God for the future generation, he can be so only insofar as he is able to make the compassion of God with man — which has become visible in Jesus Christ — credible in his own world.

The compassionate man stands in the midst of his people but does not get caught in the conformistic forces of the peer-group, because through his compassion he is able to avoid the distance of pity as well as the exclusiveness of sympathy. Compassion is born when we discover in the center of our own existence not only that God is God and man is man, but also that our neighbor is really our fellowman.

Through compassion it is possible to recognize man's craving for love in our own heart and his cruelty in our own impulses, to see our hope for forgiveness in our friend's eyes and our refusal in their bitter mouths. When they kill, we know that we could have done it; when they give life, we know that we can do the same. For a compassionate man nothing human is alien: no joy and no sorrow, no way of living and no way of dying.

This compassion is authority because it does not tolerate the pressures of the in-group, but breaks through the boundaries between languages and countries, rich and poor, educated and primitives and pulls man away from the fearful clique into the large world where he can see that every human face is the face of a fellowman. This means that the authority of compassion is the possibility of man to forgive his brother. Because forgiveness is only real for him who has discovered the weakness of his friends and the sins of his enemy in his own heart and is willing to call every human being his brother. A fatherless generation looks for brothers who are able to take away their fear and anxiety, who can open the doors of their narrow-mindedness and show them that forgiveness is a possibility which dawns on the horizon of humanity.

The compassionate man who points to the possibility of forgiveness, helps man to free himself from the chains of his restrictive shame, allows him to experience his own guilt and restores his hope for a future in which the lamb and the lion can sleep together.

Henry Nouwen
"Generation without Fathers" (pp. 49-50)

EXPERIENCING YOUR DARK SIDE

Expression of what we find within ourselves, honest and reck-
less expression before the face of the Eternal, assuming responsibility for what we are, even if we are unaware of it, and asking
God to help us to master the wild horses, or to revive the skeletons
of horses which we dig out during the long hours of our confessions — this is the psychological method of religious self-
education. It is a way of bringing to consciousness our unconscious contents, and of establishing control over our hidden
powers. It is the way to mature responsibility. It is the old way of
the Psalmist: "Yet who can detect his lapses? Absolve me from
my faults unknown! And hold thy servant back from wilful sins,
from giving way to them? (Psalm 19: 12, 13, *Moffatt*).

Not in the presence of a minister or a psychologist, but in the
presence of God, things change completely. If you hate your
brother, and you pour out all your hatred, remembering at the
same time, as much as you can, the presence of God — and your
hatred does not change, then you are not sufficiently aware
either of the presence of God or of your hatred, and probably of
neither. Be more honest, give vent to your emotions. You hate
your brother: imagine his presence, before God tell him how you
feel, kick him, scratch him. You are ten years old now — get up
from your chair, don't pretend to be a wise old Buddha, pace the
floor, yell, scream, punch the furniture, express yourself. Rant
and rage until you are exhausted, or until you laugh at
yourself.

> Fritz Kunkel
> *In Search of Maturity* (pp. 253- 254)

NAMING YOUR DARK SIDE

In the naming of the daimonic, there is an obvious and interesting parallel to the power of naming in contemporary medical and
psychological therapy. At some time, everyone must have been

aware of how relieved he was when he went to the doctor with a troublesome illness and the doctor pronounced a *name* for it. A name for the virus or germ, a name for the disease process, and the doctor could then make a statement or two about the disease on the basis of this name.

Now something deeper is going on in this phenomenon than our relief at whether or not the doctor can predict a quick cure. Or any cure, for that matter. Some years ago, after weeks of undetermined illness, I heard from a specialist that my sickness was tuberculosis. I was, I recall, distinctly relieved, *even though I was fully aware that this meant, in those days, that medicine could do nothing to cure the disease*. A number of explanations will leap to the reader's mind. He will accuse me of being glad to be relieved from responsibility; that any patient is reassured when he has the authority of the doctor to which he can give himself up; and the naming of the disorder takes away the mystery of it. But these explanations are surely too simple. Even the last one — that the naming reduces the mystery — will be seen, on further thought, as an illusion: to me the bacillus or the virus or the germ is still as much a mystery as ever, and the tubular bacillus was then still a mystery to the doctor.

The relief, rather, comes from the *act of confronting the daimonic world of illness by means of the names*. The doctor and I stand together, he knowing more names in this purgatory than I and therefore technically my guide into hell. Diagnosis (from *dia-gignoskein,* literally "knowing through") may be thought of, on one side, as our modern form of calling the name of the offending demon. Not that the rational information about the disease is unimportant; but the rational data given to me add up to something more significant than the information itself. It becomes, for me, a symbol of a change to a new way of life. The names are symbols of a certain attitude I must take toward this daimonic situation of illness; the disorder expresses a myth (a total pattern of life) which communicates to me a way in which I must now orient and order my life. This is so whether it is for two weeks with a cold or twelve years with tuberculosis; the *quantity* of time is not the point. It is a quality of life. In short, the image by which I identify myself changes by its contact with the myth portraying the daimonic in the natural processes of disease. If I overcome the disease, I shall partly be a new being, and I could rightly be initiated into a new community and be given a new name.

> Rollo May
> *Love and Will* (pp. 172-173)

SELF-KNOWLEDGE

There is a sentimentalism in the air which has told us that our identity is really to be found in what we should call the "true self." The implication is that this might better be called the "beautiful self." ... According to this way of looking at things, we have only found ourselves, and established contact with ourselves and our identities, when we are in touch with our healthy and beautiful wishes and thoughts. On the surface this is an attractive doctrine with which I am tempted to agree. But I do not. For contact with the self means contact, in increasing directness, with *whatever* is there. Of course self-knowledge is difficult and painful. But I think that all the talk in our culture about self-knowledge and especially the knowledge of the non-romantic elements in our humanity, moves too far in the direction of the pain of it all, and not nearly enough in the direction of the happiness that can come from it. Compared to this knowing, the not knowing, the loss of contact — even the loss of contact with the destructive elements in us — is like an agony compared to a pleasure. This true, sweet self is a dream that forbids membership in our humanity to anything else but itself. It makes contact with more and more of the human self impossible. It constantly proclaims that a good person would never have this thought or that feeling. It assures us that a good man or a good woman would never feel anger or despair, or think of suicide. It makes impossible that recognition which is the prelude to acceptance and mastery of these things. This is the ideal self, out of contact with the self, which excludes every sick element from its holy membership. It knows neither Jew nor gentile, nor black, nor any strong feeling about anything. It is simply beautiful.

William F. Lynch
Images of Hope (p. 184)

CONFESSING

... when he had failed in his duty, he simply confessed his fault, saying to God, *I shall never do otherwise if Thou leavest me to myself; it is Thou who must hinder my falling, and mend what is amiss.* That after this he gave himself no further uneasiness about it.

- - - - - -

... as for the miseries and sins he heard of daily in the world, he was so far from wondering at them that, on the contrary, he was surprised that there were not more, considering the malice sinners were capable of; that, for his part, he prayed for them; but knowing that God could remedy the mischiefs they did, when He pleased, he gave himself no further trouble.

- - - - - -

... he expected, after the pleasant days God had given him, he should have his turn of pain and suffering; but that he was not uneasy about it, knowing very well that as he could do nothing of himself, God would not fail to give him the strength to bear it.

- - - - - -

... he was very sensible of his faults, but not discouraged by them; that he confessed them to God, but did not plead against Him to excuse them. When he had so done, he peaceably resumed his usual practice of love and adoration.

- - - - - -

... the worst that could happen to him would be to lose that sense of God which he had enjoyed so long; but that the goodness of God assured him that He would not forsake him utterly, and that He would give him strength to bear whatever evil He permitted to happen to him; and therefore that he feared nothing ...

Brother Lawrence
His Letters and Conversations on the Practice of the Presence of God

AWAKENING

Advent is the time for rousing. Man is shaken to the very depths, so that he may wake up to the truth of himself. The primary condition for a fruitful and rewarding Advent is renunciation, surrender. Man must let go of all his mistaken dreams, his conceited poses and arrogant gestures, all the pretences with which he hopes to deceive himself and others. If he fails to do this, stark reality may take hold of him and rouse him forcibly in a way that will entail both anxiety and suffering.

The kind of awakening that literally shocks man's whole being is part and parcel of the Advent idea. A deep emotional experience like this is necessary to kindle the inner light which confirms the blessing and the promise of the Lord. A shattering awakening; that is the necessary preliminary. Life only begins when the whole framework is shaken. There can be no proper preparation without this. It is precisely in the shock of rousing while he is still deep in the helpless, semiconscious state, in the pitiable weakness of that borderland between sleep and waking, that man finds the golden thread which binds earth to heaven and gives the benighted soul some inkling of the fullness it is capable of realizing and is called upon to realize.

Alfred Delp, S.J.
The Prison Meditations of Father Delp (p. 17)

WHAT STOPS YOUR CONFESSION?

Nevertheless many even of the authorities believed in him, but for fear of the Pharisees they did not confess it, lest they should be put out of the synagogue: for they loved the praise of men more than the praise of God.

John 12:42-43, *RSV*

CONFRONTING YOURSELF

True, whoever looks into the mirror of the water will see first of all his own face. Whoever goes to himself risks a confrontation with himself. The mirror does not flatter, it faithfully shows whatever looks into it; namely, the face we never show to the world because we cover it with the *persona,* the mask of the actor. But the mirror lies behind the mask and shows the true face.

This confrontation is the first test of courage on the inner way, a test sufficient to frighten off most people, for the meeting with ourselves belongs to the more unpleasant things that can be avoided so long as we can project everything negative into the environment. But if we are able to see our own shadow and can bear knowing about it, then a small part of the problem has already been solved: we have at least brought up the personal unconscious.

C. G. Jung
The Archetypes and the Collective Unconscious, vol. 9, Collected Works (p. 20)

ACKNOWLEDGING YOUR SHADOW-SIDE

And indeed it is a frightening thought that man also has a shadow-side to him, consisting not just of little weaknesses and foibles, but of a positively demonic dynamism. The individual seldom knows anything of this; to him as an individual, it is incredible that he should ever in any circumstances go beyond himself. But let these harmless creatures form a mass, and there emerges a raging monster; and each individual is only one tiny cell in the monster's body, so that for better or worse he must accompany it on its bloody rampages and even assist it to the utmost. Having a dark suspicion of these grim possibilities, man turns a blind eye to the shadow-side of human nature. Blindly he strives against the salutary dogma of original sin, which is yet so prodigiously true. Yes, he even hesitates to admit the conflict of which he is so painfully aware.

C. G. Jung
Two Essays on Analytical Psychology, vol. 7, Collected Works (p. 30)

ACCEPTING YOUR SHADOW-SIDE

It is, indeed, very necessary to be aware of our shadow for we cannot get rid of a part of the psyche by repressing it any more than we can get rid of a part of the body by ignoring its existence. If we could really see our own shadow, it would be clear to us that in the depths of our own hearts we are not entirely the exemplary citizens we have always liked to believe ourselves. This is a very disturbing realization, and for the sake of the solidarity of society many people consider it necessary not to allow themselves to indulge in such subversive thoughts. And as it takes a great deal of moral courage to confront the shadow, it is far better, or so society itself believes, for us to throw a little dust in our own eyes in order to maintain our self-respect and good form. The dissenting voice of conscience can usually be silenced by some general form of self-depreciation such as by saying, "Well, of course I am not perfect. Who is?" And the Church provides the General Confession, but it is so very general that particular sins can slip by unnoticed. We are reminded of the man at the weekly prayer meeting whose prayer went something like this: "O Lord, I confess my sins. I have greatly sinned. I am the greatest of sinners, O Lord. I have been mean in my business dealings, for I am a great sinner; I have been angry without cause, for I am a great sinner," and much more to the same effect. Of course, everyone was greatly edified, and the man himself could not conceal his smug expression. But when his neighbor began to pray, saying "Yes, O Lord, what Brother X has just said is quite true; he is mean and cussed," Brother X sprang to his feet, shouting, "How dare you say such a thing about me? There isn't a word of truth in it! You — slanderer!"

- - - - - -

It is relatively easy to confess a sin compatible, as it were, with one's dignity or ego self-respect, while the real sin lurks unrecognized underneath.

- - - - - -

It is by no means always easy to discover where the real guilt lies. For it may not be a particular disobedience against the divine or the social ordinance, nor a particular injury to the neighbor, nor indeed a particular blunder of forgetfulness that is the real sin. It may be rather the power attitude underlying the overt act, the inveterate egotism that denies the very existence of others as persons. It is this that makes up the blackness of the shadow. In other words, when one is enclosed in one's own *Umwelt,* one is constantly sinning against the neighbor. One feels and acts as if one were the only *real* person, the others being merely wraiths. The darkness of the shadow falls on everyone else; the others seem to be the ones at fault. But when one accepts one's shadow, instead of feeling an absolute assurance that the other person is in the wrong, one may be able to recognize that the difficulty can have come from one's own unconsciousness.

In any human situation where one is really concerned to make a working relationship, it is most important to recognize the shadow. The evil that emanates from one's own psyche is in some measure under one's own control; at least one can do something about it; but the darkness that comes from the other person's unconscious is not accessible even to one's best intentioned efforts. However, since it takes two to make a quarrel, it is possible that if one clears up one's own end of the difficulty, the other person may be able to accept his shadow, too.

M. Esther Harding
The 'I' and the 'Not-I'
(pp. 87, 95, 97)

LOVING YOUR SHADOW-SIDE

I may love to the uttermost outwardly, but should the vertical connection to the ground of being within myself, to my love of myself, toward myself, by myself, not yet be formed, I will have stirred up a love that cannot please . . . the human encounter depends on an inner connection. To be in touch with you I need to be in touch within.

- - - - - -

Forced intimacy, in groups for instance, usually drives into deeper concealment those parts of the soul which can be shared only where two or three come together, not a multitude.

- - - - - -

Loving oneself is no easy matter just because it means loving all of oneself, including the shadow where one is inferior and socially so unacceptable. The care one gives this humiliating part is also the cure. More: as the cure depends on care, so does caring sometimes mean nothing more than carrying. The first essential in redemption of the shadow is the ability to carry it along with you, as did the old Puritans, or the Jews in endless exile, daily aware of their sins, watching for the Devil, on guard lest they slip, a long existential trek with a pack of rocks on the back, with no one on whom to unload it and no sure goal at the end. Yet this carrying and caring cannot be programmatic, in order to develop, in order that the inferiority comply with the ego's goals, for this is hardly love.

Loving the shadow may begin with carrying it, but even that is not enough. At one moment something else must break through, that laughing insight at the paradox of one's own folly which is also everyman's. Then may come the joyful acceptance of the rejected and inferior, a going with it and even a partial living of it. This love may even lead to an identification with and acting-out of the shadow, falling into its fascination. Therefore the moral dimension can never be abandoned. Thus is cure a paradox requiring two incommensurables: the moral recognition that these parts of me are burdensome and intolerable and must change, and the loving laughing acceptance which takes them just as they are, joyfully, forever. One both tries hard and lets go, both judges harshly and joins gladly. Western moralism and Eastern abandon: each holds only one side of the truth.

James Hillman
Insearch: Psychology and Religion
(pp. 36-67, 39, 76-77)

FACING THE TRUTH OF YOURSELF

It is the nature of self-esteem and of the human self to love only oneself and to consider oneself alone. But what can a man do? He will not be able to prevent the object of his affection from being full of faults and wretchedness; he wants to be great and finds that he is small; he wants to be happy and finds that he is unhappy; he wants to be perfect and finds that he is riddled with imperfections; he wants to be the object of man's affection and esteem and sees that his faults deserve only their dislike and contempt. The embarrassing position in which he finds himself produces in him the most unjust and criminal passion that can possibly be imagined; he conceives a mortal hatred of the truth which brings him down to earth and convinces him of his faults. He would like to be able to annihilate it and not being able to de-

stroy it in itself, he destroys it, in so far as he can, in his own mind
and in the minds of other people; that is to say, he concentrates all
his efforts on concealing his faults both from others and from
himself, and cannot stand being made to see them or their being
seen by other people.

- - - - - -

There are different degrees in this dislike of the truth; but it can
be said that it exists to some extent in all of us because it is
inseparable from self-esteem. It is this bad kind of delicacy which
forces those who feel bound to reprove other people to choose so
many devious ways and compromises to avoid shocking them.
They are obliged to make light of our faults, to appear to condone
them, to throw in praise, protestations of affection and regard.
Yet in spite of everything, it remains a bitter pill to our self-
esteem. It takes as little of the medicine as it can; it always does so
with disgust and often even with a secret ill feeling towards those
who administer it.

It thus happens that if anyone wants to make himself popular
with us, he avoids rendering a service that he knows we should
find disagreeable; he treats us as we wish to be treated; we hate
the truth and people hide it from us; we want to be flattered, and
people flatter us; we want to be deceived, and people deceive
us.

Blaise Pascal
Pensées (No. 100)

EXPERIENCING GOD THROUGH OTHERS

Who can give us the certainty that, in the confession and the
forgiveness of our sins, we are not dealing with ourselves but
with the living God? God gives us this certainty through our
brother. Our brother breaks the circle of self-deception. A man
who confesses his sins in the presence of a brother knows that he
is no longer alone with himself; he experiences the presence of
God in the reality of the other person. As long as I am by myself in
the confession of my sins, everything remains in the dark, but in

the presence of a brother the sin has to be brought into the light . . .

Our brother has been given me that even here and now I may be made certain through him of the reality of God in His judgment and His grace. As the open confession of my sins to a brother insures me against self-deception, so, too, the assurance of forgiveness becomes fully certain to me only when it is spoken by a brother in the name of God. Mutual, brotherly confession is given to us by God in order that we may be sure of divine forgiveness.

But it is precisely for the sake of this certainty that confession should deal with *concrete* sins. People usually are satisfied when they make a general confession. But one experiences the utter perdition and corruption of human nature, in so far as this ever enters into experience at all, when one sees his own specific sins . . .

Does all this mean that confession to a brother is a divine law? No, confession is not a law, it is an offer of divine help for the sinner. It is possible that a person may by God's grace break through to certainty, new life, the Cross, and fellowship without benefit of confession to a brother. It is possible that a person may never know what it is to doubt his own forgiveness and despair of his own confession of sin, that he may be given everything in his own private confession to God. We have spoken here for those who cannot make this assertion.

Dietrich Bonhoeffer
Life Together (pp. 116-117)

TRANSFORMATION

"Come now, let us reason together,"
    says the Lord:
"though your sins are like scarlet,
    they shall be as white as snow;
though they are red like crimson,
    they shall become like wool."

Isaiah 1:18, *RSV*

EXERCISE 2:

Acknowledging and Accepting Your Light Side

This exercise is to help you become more conscious of those qualities in yourself that you would want others to know about — "light" qualities as opposed to "dark" qualities. As you meditate and become aware of these "light" qualities, keep a list of them in a journal or notebook. Become acquainted with your own response to these positive parts of your self. Do you have difficulty accepting or acknowledging them? Does it make you feel self-conscious to speak of them? Do you belittle your accomplishments, lest you appear to lack modesty? Do you feel awkward when complimented and disclaim any success? Do you fear that if you confess your strengths new demands will be made of you?

Consider what may be keeping you from expressing — with abandonment — warmth, tenderness, concern, interest, generosity, praise, and those other qualities you admire. Perhaps you may even feel a total lack of these qualities. Recall those negative aspects you listed in Exercise 1 and know that each has its opposite in you. Did you list greed? Then be alert for the generous impulse. Did you list envy? Then look for that self in you which makes the response of praise. Consider the circumstances or feelings which block your expression of the admirable qualities.

Be so bold as to write your own "Song of Myself" with Walt Whitman's words for inspiration:

> *I celebrate myself, and sing myself,*
> *And what I assume, you shall assume,*
> *For every atom belonging to me as good belongs to you.*

Celebrate yourself. Confess the person whom you are becoming in Christ. This is the confession of your light side. Many people find it easier to dig and probe the dark dimension of life than to come to grips with the resources that are theirs. When we do not recognize our gifts and strengths, our lives fail to sound notes of gratitude. The whole growth process is blocked. We are responsible and free only when we acknowledge our resources and the fact that light has actually penetrated our darkness and made us children of light. Where sin did abound, grace does much more abound.

Our fundamental confession is who we are in Christ. The deepest confession anyone will ever make is this: I am a person in Christ Jesus. He has confronted me. His power has begun to flow into my life. I am a changed and changing creation. I am his, and I can witness to his grace and power, and to the strength and possibilities that are mine because of him.

THE CALL TO CREATIVITY

It is absurd to charge me with an attempt to defy God. Creativity for me is implied in the fundamental Christian truth of God-manhood, and its justification is the theandric theme of Christianity. God's idea of man is infinitely loftier than traditional orthodox conceptions of man, which are as often as not an expression of a frustrated and stunted mind. The idea of God is the greatest human idea, and the idea of man is the greatest divine idea. Man awaits the birth of God in himself, and God awaits the birth of man in himself. It is at this level that the question of creativity arises, and it is from this point of view that it should be approached. The notion that God has need of man and of man's response to him is, admittedly, an extraordinarily daring notion; yet in its absence the Christian revelation of God-manhood loses all meaning. The drama of God and his Other One, Man, is present and operative in the very depths of divine life. This is revealed not in theological doctrines but in spiritual experience, where the divine drama passes into a human drama and that which is above is converted into that which is below. But this is in no way inconsistent with redemption: rather it is another moment on the same spiritual path and another act in the mystical drama of God and man.

- - - - - -

As I have noted, I passed through a phase of the crushing experience of sin, and in the wake of this experience darkness gathered around me. Had I followed this path to the end, unable to dispel its evil charm, I should have grown accustomed to a perpetual contemplation of sin, to a brooding over darkness, rather than to a vision of light. It is, in fact, the aim of religious life to put an end to this oppressive attitude. The sense of dejection and lowness of spirit gave way in me to a sense of exultation. I can remember how one summer day just before dawn I was suddenly seized by a tumultuous force which seemed to wrench me away from the oppressive spell of my despondent condition, and a light invaded my whole being. I knew then that this was the exalting

call to creativity: henceforth I would create out of the freedom of
my soul like the great artificer whose image I bear.

Nicolas Berdyaev
Dream and Reality
(pp. 204-205, 205-206)

THE RESPONSIBILITY TO USE YOUR GIFTS

Why? Why are we afraid to embrace our virtues? Why do we
mask them behind inaccurate estimates and unreasonable fears?
Sometimes we may unconsciously reject our hidden powers
because they are linked with impulses that are unacceptable
either to ourselves or to the society in which we set our lives. But
the more common answer is a much simpler one. Basically, we
resist recognition of our assets because, once recognized, they
must be *used*.

For goodness makes claims. It must be expressed. It must be
used. Otherwise, it becomes evil in our hands. Badness is goodness dammed up, just as hell is heaven dammed up. The man who
knows he could help others but helps only himself will ultimately
not be able to live with himself. He will be his own worst tormen-
tor. The man who knows he could heal people but is afraid to risk
the sacrifice, responsibility, and hardship — as well as the hum-
bling knowledge that sometimes he will not be able to heal — is
ultimately victimized by his own unfulfillment. The man who
will not accept the risk of loving and receiving love will live and
die in emptiness.

Literature is full of stories of people who knew they had talent,
yet failed to use it. The untold stories are those of the millions of
individuals who unconsciously disguised their virtues lest they
be obliged to use them — and lost the riches of true living in the
process. In this one sense, we human beings are akin to the bat-
tery in a flashlight; unused, it corrodes. What we do not use is
wasted; what we do not share we cannot keep.

Earl A. Loomis, Jr.
The Self in Pilgrimage (pp. 6-7)

STAYING TRUE TO YOUR INNER NATURE

The serious thing for each person to recognize vividly and poignantly, each for himself, is that every falling away from species-virtue, every crime against one's own nature, every evil act, *every one without exception records itself* in our unconscious and makes us despise ourselves. Karen Horney had a good word to describe this unconscious perceiving and remembering; she said it "registers." If we do something we are ashamed of, it "registers" to our discredit, and if we do something honest or fine or good, it "registers" to our credit. The net results ultimately are either one or the other — either we respect and accept ourselves or we despise ourselves and feel contemptible, worthless, and unlovable. Theologians used to use the word *"accidie"* to describe the sin of failing to do with one's life all that one knows one could do.

- - - - - -

But there is also another element in conscience, or, if you like, another kind of conscience, which we all have either weakly or strongly. And this is the "intrinsic conscience." This is based upon the unconscious and preconscious perception of our own nature, of our own destiny, or our own capacities, of our own "call" in life. It insists that we be true to our inner nature and that we do not deny it out of weakness or for advantage or for any other reason. He who belies his talent, the born painter who sells stockings instead, the intelligent man who lives a stupid life, the man who sees the truth and keeps his mouth shut, the coward who gives up his manliness, all these people perceive in a deep way that they have done wrong to themselves and despise themselves for it. Out of this self-punishment may come only neurosis, but there may equally well come renewed courage, righteous indignation, increased self-respect, because of thereafter doing the right thing; in a word, growth and improvement can come through pain and conflict.

- - - - - -

We can no longer think of the person as "fully determined" where this phrase implies "determined only by forces external to the person." The person, insofar as he *is* a real person, is his own main determinant. Every person is, in part, "his own project" and makes himself.

- - - - - -

Intrinsic guilt is the consequence of betrayal of one's own inner nature or self, a turning off the path to self-actualization, and is essentially justified self-disapproval. It is therefore not as culturally relative as is Freudian guilt. It is "true" or "deserved" or "right and just" or "correct" because it is a discrepancy from something profoundly real within the person rather than from accidental, arbitrary or purely relative localisms. Seen in this way it is good, even *necessary,* for a person's development to have intrinsic guilt when he deserves to. It is not just a symptom to be avoided at any cost but is rather an inner guide for growth toward actualization of the real self, and of its potentialities.

Abraham H. Maslow
Toward a Psychology of Being
(pp. 5, 7, 193, 194-195)

GIVING YOUR POTENTIAL ROOM TO GROW

The primary atmosphere in which the human being lives and moves and has his being is inward. It is contained in the way a person thinks about himself, perceives and experiences his fundamental nature. It involves his conception of himself, his potentialities, and the resources upon which he can draw. These comprise the atmosphere of his life, and they are within him. But they are not only internal individually; they are within the depths of persons in a way that reaches across the community. The inward atmosphere of a civilization is a social fact that is expressed psychologically in the individuals who comprise the culture. The task of improving the quality of a civilization must therefore be approached in terms of the individual in the culture and his personal experience of meaning, or lack of meaning in life.

In the seed there is the latent potentiality of development that carries all the possibilities of what the full grown species can become. Following this metaphor, the fullness of the oak trees is latent in the acorn. It is implicit there, and correspondingly, the depths of man, his *unconscious,* is the carrier of human potentialities. It contains the possibilities of human development that are present in the individual but are not visible because they have not yet become manifest in life. We cannot see them until they begin to unfold and fulfill themselves in the world. For this, it is necessary that the individual develop the capacity of perceiving the inward process of his growth while it is still in motion and before it is fulfilled. As he becomes sensitive to it and attunes himself to the process of his growth inwardly, he is able to draw his potentialities forward. To provide the methodology for this is a primary task of depth psychology.

- - - - - -

While this sensitivity to the inward process is being developed, a particular attitude is called for on the part of the depth psychologist himself. This is an attitude of connection to the seed of the other person, an acceptance of it without defining it (so as not to limit its potentiality by his own preconceptions), and a sensitive openness to the process by which it is unfolding. In a profound sense this is an attitude of love, for it involves an affirmation of the seed of potentiality in the other person *even while that seed has not disclosed its specific form.*

Ira Progoff
The Symbolic and the Real (pp. 12, 21-22, 61-62)

DRAWING ON YOUR RESOURCES

In a word, man need neither capitulate to nature nor defy it in order to be himself. The tragic struggle whereby he seeks to come to terms with life and destiny is not a lonely, transitory one, wherein for a brief period he creates *ex nihilo* whatever humane meaning existence can possess; for this struggle is an integral part of a cosmic creativity. The buried resources are "there," so that they can be drawn upon, only because of a divine strategy which reaches back beyond the appearance of man upon this planet. Man is in his own body and mind a compendium of every preceding "level" of evolution — physical, chemical, biological and psychological. The resources he draws upon, in seeking to become at one with himself, are not merely "his"; they are rooted in the whole creation, which is grounded in God. Therefore man can become at one with himself only by finding his place in a harmony much wider than himself; but this harmony is not "preestablished"; he has a share in winning, in actualizing, it. He cannot fulfill his own nature unless his capacities gain free expression; but neither can he fulfill his own nature unless his freedom is brought into right relationship with God.

David E. Roberts
Psychotherapy and a Christian View of Man (p. 93)

FOLLOWING YOUR HEART

There are, besides the gifts of the head, also those of the heart, which are no whit less important, although they may easily be overlooked because in such cases the head is often the weaker organ. And yet people of this kind sometimes contribute more to the well-being of society, and are more valuable, than those with other talents.

C. G. Jung
The Development of Personality, vol. 17, Collected Works (p. 140)

THE COURAGE TO LET GO

Man is always torn between the wish to regress to the womb and the wish to be fully born. Every act of birth requires the courage to let go of something, to let go of the womb, to let go of the breast, to let go of the lap, to let go of the hand, to let go eventually of all certainties, and to rely only upon one thing: one's own powers to be aware and to respond; that is, one's own creativity. To be creative means to consider the whole process of life as a process of birth, and not to take any stage of life as a final stage. Most people die before they are fully born. Creativeness means to be born before one dies.

The willingness to be born — and this means the willingness to let go of all "certainties" and illusions — requires *courage* and *faith.* Courage to let go of certainties, courage to be different and to stand isolation; courage, as the Bible puts it in the story of Abraham, to leave one's own land and family and to go to a land yet unknown. Courage to be concerned with nothing but the truth, the truth not only in thought but in one's feeling as well. This courage is possible only on the basis of faith. Faith not in the sense in which the word is often used today, as a belief in some idea which cannot be proved scientifically or rationally, but faith in the meaning which it has in the *Old Testament,* where the word for faith (Emuna) means certainty; to be certain of the reality of one's own experience in thought and in feeling, to be able to trust it, to rely on it, this is faith. Without courage and faith, creativity is impossible, and hence the understanding and cultivation of courage and faith are indispensable conditions for the development of the creative attitude.

Let me say again that creativity in this sense does not refer to a quality which particularly gifted persons or artists could achieve, but to an attitude which every human being should and can achieve. Education for creativity is nothing short of education for living.

Erich Fromm
"The Creative Attitude"
Creativity and Its Cultivation (pp. 53-54)

EXPLORING YOUR POTENTIALITIES

For the self-renewing man the development of his own potentialities and the process of self-discovery never end. It is a sad but
unarguable fact that most human beings go through their lives
only partially aware of the full range of their abilities. As a boy in
California I spent a good deal of time in the Mother Lode country,
and like every boy of my age I listened raptly to the tales told by
the old-time prospectors in that area, some of them veterans of
the Klondike gold rush. Every one of them had at least one good
campfire story of a lost gold mine. The details varied: the original
discoverer had died in the mine, or had gone crazy, or had been
killed in the shooting scrape, or had just walked off thinking the
mine worthless. But the central theme was constant: riches left
untapped. I have come to believe that those tales offer a paradigm
of education as most of us experience it. The mine is worked for a
little while and then abandoned.

- - - - - -

Exploration of the full range of his own potentialities is not
something that the self-renewing man leaves to the chances of
life. It is something he pursues systematically, or at least avidly,
to the end of his days. He looks forward to an endless and
unpredictable dialogue between his potentialities and the claims
of life — not only the claims he encounters but the claims he
invents. And by potentialities I mean not just skills but the full
range of his capacities for sensing, wondering, learning, understanding, loving and aspiring.

John W. Gardner
Self-Renewal (pp. 10, 12)

INNER UNITY

The words in the Scriptures: "But ye that did cleave unto the
Lord your God are alive every one of you this day," are expounded as follows:

"Cleave to his qualities." But this must be properly understood. Emanating from God are ten qualities and these come in twos which oppose each other like two colors, one of which is apparently in direct contrast to the other. But, seen with the true inner eye, they all form one simple unity. It is the task of man to make them appear a unity to the true outer eye, as well. Perhaps one man finds it difficult to be merciful, because his way is to be rigorous, and another finds it difficult to be rigorous, because his way is merciful. But he who binds the rigor within him to its root, to the rigor of God, and the mercy which is in him to its root, to the mercy of God, and so on in all things — such a man will unite the ten qualities within himself, and he himself will become the unity they represent, for he cleaves to the Lord of the world. Such a man has become wax on which both judgment and mercy can set their seal.

> Martin Buber
> *Ten Rungs: Hasidic Sayings*
> (pp. 70-71)

FOCUSING ON THE GOOD

Finally, brethren, whatever is true, whatever is honorable, whatever is just, whatever is pure, whatever is lovely, whatever is gracious, if there is any excellence, if there is anything worthy of praise, think about these things. What you have learned and received and heard and seen in me, do; and the God of peace will be with you.

> Phillippians 4:8-9, *RSV*

THE COST OF NEGLECTING YOUR SELF

Not following one's destiny, or trying to avoid one's fate, is a frequent cause of numerous psychic difficulties. It may even be that the steady increase in the number of neurotics today is due to the fact that more and more individuals are called upon by fate to work for their psychic wholeness, but that fewer and fewer of them are ready to do so. Any obstruction of the natural process of development, any avoidance of the law of life, or getting stuck on a level unsuited to one's age, takes its revenge, if not immediately, then later at the onset of the second half of life, in the form of serious crises, nervous breakdowns, and all manner of physical and psychic sufferings. Mostly they are accompanied by vague feelings of guilt, by tormenting pangs of conscience, often not understood, in the face of which the individual is helpless. He knows he is not guilty of any bad deed, he has not given way to any illicit impulse, and yet he is plagued by uncertainty, discontent, despair, and above all by anxiety — a constant, indefinable anxiety. And in truth he must usually be pronounced "guilty." His guilt does not lie in the fact that he has a neurosis, but in the fact that, knowing he has one, he does nothing to set about curing it.

This also explains why many practising Catholics do not feel freed by confession and absolution, but go on being oppressed and persecuted by fears. And indeed they cannot confess anything except what lies consciously on their conscience, while they are not conscious of their real guilt at all; it is not anything they have done or thought, essentially it is ungraspable and can hardly be put into words. For it relates to their whole previous life, to which they did not pay its due tribute; it relates to the "destiny" that was laid upon them but was not lived, to the psychic development they missed, which their nature would yet have made possible. The fact that they remained infantile, their onesidedness and the neglect of their other qualities, their fear of taking the plunge into life, their constant prevarication and criticism — all this and a lot more besides are the cause of guilt feelings and pangs of conscience which never let them go.

Jolande Jacobi
The Way of Individuation
(pp. 115-116)

GROWTH OF YOUR HIDDEN SELF

This, then, is what I pray, kneeling before the Father, from whom every family, whether spiritual or natural, takes its name:

Out of his infinite glory, may he give you the power through his Spirit for your hidden self to grow strong, so that Christ may live in your hearts through faith, and then, planted in love and built on love, you will with all the saints have strength to grasp the breadth and the length, the height and the depth; until, knowing the love of Christ, which is beyond all knowledge, you are filled with the utter fullness of God.

Glory be to him whose power, working in us, can do infinitely more than we can ask or imagine; glory be to him from generation to generation in the Church and in Christ Jesus for ever and ever. Amen.

Ephesians 3: 14-21, *Jer.*

PRAYER
AND A COFFEE HOUSE

PRAYER
AND A COFFEE HOUSE

PRAYER AND COMMUNITY

When a house is a house of prayer, the atmosphere of it is different. Many of us have seen this first hand working in The Potter's House, the coffee house/bookstore which The Church of The Saviour has operated in the inner city of Washington, D.C., for the past twenty-six years. The people who have come through the doors have told us in many ways that they sense this is not an ordinary coffee house. Some fall silent when they enter the room, and walk softly to their tables. Others are more casual, but go to great lengths to account for the tone of the coffee house. One customer will say that it is the old barn boards nailed to the walls that create the stillness of forests, while another will insist that the worn carpeting or the current art exhibit is what "really makes this place." Almost everything in the large room has been pointed out at one time or another to explain the feeling that people have about the coffee house.

Those of us who work at The Potter's House respond in different ways at different times. Our reactions are determined by what is going on in the corporate life of the group which staffs The Potter's House on any given night, as well as by what is happening in our private worlds. If there is dissension in the group and unresolved conflict among members, the Spirit of the coffee house leaves, and in the place of it is a covering of darkness. Fortunately, on those nights when there is a lack of unity in us and among us, not many people seem to come to the coffee house. It is as though a protective wall were thrown up around The Potter's House and only certain people allowed to go through it.

Some of us first noted this when the mission group which staffs The Potter's House on Friday nights set aside a "community table" for those who came alone and wanted to meet people. When all was well with us as a group, the table would fill up quickly and there would be the exhilarating experience of exciting conversation and real meeting between persons. But when, in our time together before the coffee house opened, we had quarreled among ourselves and moved perfunctorily through forms of worship and prayer, the mere thought of the "community table" loomed as burden. No one wanted to be assigned there, either to take coffee orders or to act as greeter for part of the evening. It was a fruitless obligation to try to relate to strangers when we were relating so poorly to our own group members. Consistently, however, few people came on those nights, and the ones who did come preferred to sit alone. Under these circumstances we began to save ourselves the pain of even thinking about a community table, since there would not be community anyway.

We learned then, if we had not learned it before, that community is not programmed into an evening, but becomes possible only when there are those who have done the essential, preliminary, inward work of prayer. On the nights we labored to still our thoughts and to place ourselves, each other, and the whole evening in the presence of God, there was a communicating Spirit in the coffee house. We understood what others were saying, and they understood what we were saying. Times like these have made the coffee house an oasis in the city — a place of cool water, and peace. When the work of prayer has been done, we can see and hear in each other what otherwise comes to us distorted or is entirely blotted out. We do not have the crippling need to be confirmed by others or to struggle to find a place for ourselves in the scheme of things. Prayer frees us to be there for the other person. It is preparation for the event of community.

Of course, very few believe this. Too often we think community is dependent on the structures we create rather than on the atmosphere we create. In the secular context we think our community programs are dependent on funds and trained personnel and facilities. We do not question these assumptions even when well-staffed and funded programs never get off the ground, when money intended for the accomplishment of specific goals is used in wasteful ways, when the community organization is destroyed by internal bickering, or its energies drained in needless competition with other organizations committed to the same goals.

PRAYER AND THE MISSION OF THE CHURCH

The critics of the church's involvement in social programs may be right, if the church's involvement is on the same basis as that of non-religious organizations. Unless the church's efforts are coupled with a spiritual movement, nothing new is created. Renewal takes place in institutions when there is renewal in souls. The outpouring of the Holy Spirit and a new epoch of freedom and creativity will come when the church follows the instructions of the Risen Christ and keeps her house a house of prayer, whether that house is a day care building, a factory, or a housing project. Only then will our centers be radiating structures of light. Only then can there exist the climate for miracle or, in everyday speech, the climate for change.

As I have pondered the place of contemplative prayer in the life of the church, my thoughts have often turned back to The Potter's House, which has been for some of us the kindergarten of our instruction. If we learned there that prayer was not easy, we also learned that it was not abstract, but directly related to our perception of ourselves and each other and the world. We had read a pamphlet by Thomas Kelly, *The Gathered Meeting,* in which Kelly describes the Quaker practice of silent worship and the depth of power that steals over the worshipers:

> A blanket of divine covering comes over the room, and a quickening Presence pervades us, breaking down some part of the special privacy and isolation of our individual lives and blending our spirits within a super-individual Life and Power — an objective, dynamic Presence which enfolds us all, nourishes our souls, speaks glad, unutterable comfort within us, and quickens in us depths that had before been slumbering.[1]

One of the conditions cited by Kelly as necessary for such a group experience is that some individuals upon entering the meeting be already "gathered deep in the spirit of worship." This guidance served only as interesting reading until a feeling of desperation had brought some of us to our knees. After that we found that we came together with a new capacity to understand and care for one another, confirming in our own hearts Kelly's conviction that prayer is the proper preparation for our gatherings. Unfortunately we do not usually make that discovery until we are anxious, or have a heart full of pain.

There is a saying that a person's belief in praying for rain depends on how many days it has been since it last rained. The Potter's House Saturday night group can tell you about a long dry stretch when it lost half of its members. Too few remained to staff the evening and those few who did stay lacked commitment. Even the moderator of the group — or the Prior as we called him — was dubious that he should fill the role. With so much uncertainty in the group, it was questionable whether The Potter's House should be kept open on Saturday nights, though this was the night when it was usually the most crowded and when there were the most out-of-town visitors.

The moderator probably felt more weighted down than the others, since one of his tasks was to articulate the vision and re-sound the call when group members were under pressure or had grown fainthearted. In any case, he was the one who spent four hours one Saturday afternoon interceding for his group and asking for wisdom. It was not until he was driving to the meeting that night that he felt a resolution of the division he had been experiencing, and a unifying of his own life around the call to The Potter's House. He knew within himself the "unutterable comfort" that Thomas Kelly had described and was able to tell the group he felt called to this mission and was excited about its possibilities. At the same time his words freed others to make their own decision.

Listening to the responses of the members, one would not have suspected that anyone had been entertaining the slightest doubt concerning call. One woman who had asked for a three-month pregnancy leave even said that two weeks was all that was necessary. Since that time, the group has not only staffed The Potter's House on Saturdays with zest and abandonment, but has worked with other businesses on the street to bring renewal to the whole area. The very members, who at one point were too pressed for time to spend every Saturday evening at The Potter's House, began to meet extra hours during the week to work with the details of buying property that would provide low-cost housing for the elderly. What they had once viewed as a ridiculous burden, they now viewed as an unlimited opportunity. As you may guess, "The Lord added to their number day by day" (Acts 2:47, *RSV*).

The flux between despair and enthusiasm seems to affect different groups at different times. It takes seven mission groups to staff The Potter's House each week, and always at least one of them is somewhat down, if not completely buried in a pit of darkness. In time, even when seemingly going downhill, we learned to believe in the reality of God and to suspect that these down times may be when God is working out the new in our lives.

More than the corporate life of the various groups comes to mind, however, when I think of prayer and the mission of the church. There is the interaction of life with life that goes on day in and day out. Two stories from the on-going drama of The Potter's House will serve to illustrate.

The first is the story of a man who lived across the street from The Potter's House since it opened in 1959. In all those years he had been inside the coffee house only a dozen times, but it was to The Potter's House he turned for help when the doctors told him that he could die any day. He sent his wife to request that someone come over to talk to him about philosophy. When she returned with the message that we would come, he had her telephone and change the request to "someone who would talk about religion." He was wise enough to know that a person who can talk about philosophy is not necessarily someone who can talk about God. His message was passed on to the Sunday night mission group. Don McClanen, who had been on retreat all weekend and was alive with the Spirit in his own life, said that he would like to go. Seventeen-year old Mary Anne Cresswell said she would like to go with him. The group sent them both across the street to make the call.

They were greeted by a man who began, "I am religious by nature. I believe in Christ, but I do not go to church. I do not know how to pray. I want help in understanding the spirit that is in The Potter's House." Then he added, "But I am a realist, too. I believe in looking at things as they are. I have cancer of the most virulent kind. I'm going to die, and I want to know whether your religion has any hope and guidance to give."

Don told him that he was grateful to him for speaking so directly. "We, too, are realists," he said. "Our faith deals realistically with death."

In the next ten minutes Don talked of his own understanding of I Corinthians 15, which was the Scripture that he had worked with on retreat. It was Scripture that had acted also upon his own life. He was able to speak of the power of Christ over death because, as he told this man, "My wife and I experienced it at the time of the death of our child. There was more than sorrow, pain, disappointment, anger. There was growth, expansion of faith, a new conviction that this life is but a one-foot ruler alongside God's unending yardstick of eternity."

They talked a long time that evening. From all that we understand, the dying man, the confident proclaimer of the Word, and the eager, expectant girl had their own revival service. When Don and Mary Anne left, the man was feeling better; he also knew something about prayer and held in his hands a Book that had become more understandable, and in the days to come was to be pored over and underlined. Moreover, a man had been born into a community of hope. The Sunday night mission group became his family. They prayed for him, visited him almost daily, took books to him, and told him what Jesus Christ meant to them. They also appointed Pat Davis, the Shepherd of their group, as a special guide to help him grow in his understanding of prayer and Scripture.

Instead of dying, this man began to gain strength. In the meantime his doctors were trying to complete arrangements for him to go to a famous New York hospital where research was being done on his type of disease. Sometimes he was impatient awaiting word that he could be admitted; at other times he was not sure that he should go at all. If he was to die soon, he wanted to be at home with his new friends.

When the hospital finally sent word that they had a bed for him, he left somewhat reluctantly for New York. When he was examined at the hospital, the doctors found that the disease had been arrested. After several weeks they sent him home to resume his "normal" activities. He thought he was doing this, but no one who had known him before would have considered his activities normal. He prayed and worshiped and associated with the odd assortment of people who staffed The Potter's House on Sunday nights — people who gave as much attention to the miracle of changing life as to the miracle of physical healing.

They were realists in that group and were not sure how many days their new friend had; but then they would not have been sure about how many days you, or I, or anyone else has. They thought what mattered in God's economy is how we live those days. More than this, they thought the Sermon on the Mount was about a new life that can come to us all. They said very clearly the Sermon was about an enabling Presence that makes new life possible in the here and now.

The second story is also about an event that took place one Sunday evening. Jane Adams, the hostess at The Potter's House for the evening, approached Bill Mason, the group's Prior, whose job that night was to wait on tables. Bill was twenty-eight, but he seemed ageless; he could have been fifty or one hundred. The hostess told him that she had just seated two young men at his table. "But before that," she said, "they were in the gift area, and I think the big one took something."

"Are you sure?" asked Bill.

"It appeared that way," she said, "and he chuckled and said to his friend, 'Look what I have.' "

Confronting a customer with an accusation of theft had absolutely no appeal for Bill.

"Are you one-hundred percent sure?" he asked Jane.

"Only ninety-nine percent," she replied.

Bill shook his head, and Jane said what those of us who know Jane would expect her to say in circumstances like these: "Maybe the Spirit will lead me to sit down and talk to him."

Bill was glad for the Spirit to give her any sort of guidance as long as he was left out of it. He observed his customers, however, with more than ordinary interest as he asked them for their order. He had written it down, turned around, and walked a few steps from the table when, without any intention of doing so, he turned around, walked back to the table, and addressed the tall young man.

"One of the staff," he said, "thinks she saw you take something from the gift area."

"Nope," was the reply.

"Were you just in the gift area?"

"No."

"Then," said Bill, astounded at the words coming out of his mouth, "you wouldn't mind my looking in your pockets?"

Unexpectedly, the young man reached into his pocket and placed on the table a small art object. "You have me," he said.

With that Bill pulled a chair over to the table and sat down, not having the vaguest idea what he was going to say next.

"Why did you do it?" he asked.

"Just for kicks," was the reply. "Don't try to understand me. Do what you have to do."

It turned out that he was a college graduate doing small theater work in a nearby state. Somewhere in the conversation Bill asked the young man's companion, "What do you think about all this?"

"I wouldn't get so upset about it, if I were you," he said. "The kid's never grown up."

"What did you say to him when he took it?"

"Nothing," was the answer. "No reason for me to get involved. It's his life."

"That's just it," said Bill. " It *is* his life. If you saw him holding his hand over this candle flame and the flesh falling away, would you still do nothing? Both of you make me angry."

Bill then told them about the coffee house and its mission to the city and how every month the coffee house showed a deficit which the people of The Potter's House had to make up. "Shoplifting," said Bill, "makes it almost impossible for us to exist here."

The young man kept injecting, "This is a big learning experience for me."

Finally Bill said, "Yes, but you'll walk out of here and five minutes from now you will have forgotten it. I don't want it to be that way. I want you to have time to think about it. You have a choice: either I call the police and we go down to the station where I will sign the papers for your arrest, or you can wash dishes tonight."

"Me wash dishes?" he said. "You have to be kidding!"

His indignation, however, waned quickly. The alternative to washing dishes was too grim.

He settled nervously into his new job, but grew more at home with it as the night wore on. When closing time came and Bill went to release him, he was deeply engrossed in a book he had found in the stock room.

"You sure have some terrific books here," he said very quietly. After that he left, and curiously enough Bill felt lonely.

More could be said about these two encounters in a coffee house, but enough has been told to illustrate the constant interplay of life with life that goes on when a group is making an effort to live out of a quiet center. The experience of centered lives can be one of creativity, of a pervading Presence, of joy, of quiet contagious excitement, differing from time to time, but always issuing in community. One has the feeling of being in on what is important and wanting others to be in on it also. Most of us in the churches subscribe to the Christian message that every life is infinitely precious and unique, but the experience one has of looking out on a room full of people is different from the one-to-one encounter where one knows in one's inmost self that that message is true. Someone once put it this way: "Sometimes when I look at the people in the coffee house, I want to go up to each one of them and say, 'It does not matter *what* your opinion is. It is utterly important, simply because it *is* your opinion.' I so much want them to know that their lives count."

In contemplative prayer lies the possibility that we will hear in our depths the tidings, "for to you is born this day...a Savior" (Luke 2:11, *RSV*), and be commissioned to find ways to take that message to the distraught, hungry, imprisoned masses of a city. "Here I am, send me" (Isaiah 6:8, *Jer.*). Contemplative prayer is communion with a sphere that is beyond the world we know, but that communion makes possible an authentic, healing community in the here and now into which people can come and be renewed and find out what it is they are supposed to be doing.

Contemplative prayer is about community, and it is about being commissioned. It is going some place because one is sent, and then it is being a contemplative person in that place until one knows or is told what to do next. Much of our unease comes from not knowing where we are supposed to be. We choose one activity, think we probably made a mistake, and change to another — or we try to do everything. Sometimes we go to the other extreme and, afraid to make the wrong commitment, we make none at all. Whatever our path, we do not feel right inside.

The same dilemma is evident in the church's corporate life. The difficulty is not that the church is engaged in social programs, but that she is engaged without having been sent. After we become thoroughly involved in community action or political protest, we begin to wonder whether that is what the church should be doing after all. We are activists for a few years before we question what all the activity is accomplishing and what it has to do with the preaching of the gospel. Gradually the church pulls out of involvement altogether and returns to prayer and worship. Several more years will go by before unease begins to surface again — and this time prayer and worship will be questioned. The ambivalence that we know in our individual lives is extended to our corporate life.

It is not an either/or style of life. In fact, the contemplative life must be the foundation of all the church's missions or task forces, as well as the foundation of our individual vocations. We are twentieth- and twenty-first century people; nonetheless, we have hints that we can receive directions as clear as those given Ananias, who answered as Isaiah had answered centuries before him:

> " 'Here I am, Lord.' And the Lord said to him, 'Rise and
> go to the street called Straight, and inquire in the house
> of Judas for a man of Tarsus named Saul; for behold,
> he is praying . . .' "
>
> — Acts 9:10-11, *RSV*

When a community has listened to instructions like these and moved in obedience to them, then any arguments as to whether or not the church should be where it is are groundless. The only sensible inquiry is whether the church heard its directions correctly. We carry the treasure in earthenware vessels. The Word we say we heard is always subject to questioning, always to be tested within the fellowship and confirmed or denied by those among us who have the gift of distinguishing true spirits from false. When we become serious about prayer, we learn how important this gift is, for the contemplative person will be addressed, will be given dreams and will see visions.

PRAYER AND FASTING

After the 1968 riots in Washington, D.C., the mission groups of The Potter's House were given the vision of the City of Washington made new and habitable for all its people. With that vision came the summons to share the dream and to find the ways to labor for the building of the city. We renewed our commitment to struggle for the deepening of our prayer life, knowing that if direction and strategy were not determined by the Holy Spirit, we might as well save our energy — "Unless the Lord watches over the city, the watchman stays awake in vain" (Ps. 127:1, *RSV*).

We also increased our tithes; and — after the appearance in our midst of a visitor from another church who said, "If you will fast one day a week for two years, I promise you will not be sorry" — we added the discipline of fasting one day a week. We had asked our visitor none of the hard questions that we were accustomed to asking when faced with the extraordinary. In the presence of a person who radiated a peace from within, we believed that the promise made was the promise of gospel. We began to look again at Jesus' response to the disciples when they questioned him about their inability to cure, and he told them that there was a kind of disease that could be conquered only through prayer and fasting.

When our Potter's House mission groups met to consider adding this new discipline, we found that all of us either had individual opinions on fasting or we readily expounded someone else's opinion. But not one of us was able to speak out of personal experience.

We decided to adopt the discipline of fasting one day a week for one year, feeling that at the end of that time each person could speak experientially and decide whether it was a discipline he or she wanted to continue. The few who requested an exception for reasons of health, or because very early the effort proved too strenuous, were asked to substitute another discipline of fasting. (An acceptable substitute was the practice, one day a week, of speaking only when it was essential, and then to use the minimum of words necessary for communication. Most of us, however, kept the food fast.) Someone had the idea of giving the money we were saving on food to programs to feed the poor; many did this, although the suggestion was never adopted as a group discipline. The hunger fund grew quickly to $7,000, and The Potter's House began to serve a hot morning meal to forty school children.

That same year we became familiar with the inadequacies of the food stamp program in the District of Columbia. One of its main deficiencies was the long process necessary to become eligible for certification. The certification centers closed at the end of each day without having taken care of many people who had stood in line for hours.

Contrary to what we may imagine, hunger, poverty, and age do not motivate people to seek help, but any one of these conditions drastically lowers their capacity to endure the frustrations that seem to be built into so many unwieldy public assistance programs. Consequently, those who are most in need of food find the process of certification intolerable and in the early stages drop out.

As we became awake to the fact that the nation's capital was full of hungry people, we began to discover the hungry in our own neighborhood. One Sunday morning, news of the fasting and hunger programs of The Potter's House was shared with the larger worshiping congregation of The Church of The Saviour. I remember that day especially because ten-year-old Michael Barnet, who puts immense value on a dollar, was in the congregation. He was so moved by what was said about the plight of the poor that he dug into his pocket for his own comforting wad of two one-dollar bills and, as the collection plate went by, dropped his entire wealth into it. Later that day when his family met to discuss whether they would as a family unit adopt the fasting program and give the money to feed the poor, Michael, who is also a lover of good food, cast his vote for the fast. This family agreed on a modified plan — one day each week they would go without breakfast and lunch and would have soup and crackers for supper.

PRAYER AND ACTION

The spiritual world is full of mystery, and few of us have entered very deeply into that mystery. The relationship between money and the spiritual, however, is not so shrouded in the unknown as we would like to think. Religious literature has many stories of dedicated persons who prayed for money for worthy projects and received that money. One of the best known examples is that of George Mueller who, without any funds of his own, petitioned God day by day for the means to establish homes that would take orphaned children off the streets of London. He wrote of the establishment of his first orphanage:

"All the various arguments which I have often brought
before God, I brought also again this morning before
him. Never, during all these 14 months and 3 weeks,
have I had the least doubt that I should have all which
is requisite. — And now, dear believing reader, rejoice
and praise with me. About an hour after I had prayed
thus, there was given to me the sum of Two Thousand
Pounds for the Building Fund."[2]

There are not many stories like this in the current literature of the
church because we have become too knowledgeable to think that,
when we bow our heads and tell God about our little plans, God is
going to dispatch the resources to carry them out. The sad fact is that,
despite our sophistication, we are so naive as to suppose that George
Mueller and all those who still intercede are saying the childhood
prayers that we have outgrown. If childish petitions are honored only
in our childhood, it is because adulthood calls each of us to an ever-
deepening perception of what prayer is, and to an understanding of
the difference between a childish prayer and childlike praying. Certainly the mature person who prays for money must be as free from
its tyranny as George Mueller was. When we cling to what we have,
and spend most of our lives trying to achieve security for ourselves, it
is useless as well as immoral to go out and ask others to part with
what they cling to — that which, for them, means security.

The fight for justice is easy as long as justice is what someone else
ought to do, while our role is to pound home the message. If one
ponders the claims justice makes on one's self, the answers are not so
clearly perceived. Before becoming angry about the violence that is
done to the poor in our cities, in the institutions for children, the aged,
and the mentally ill, and the terrible violence done to two-thirds of
the world's people who go to bed hungry, we need to look first at the
violence in our own lives. For me the enemies were the rich and the
indifferent, none of whom I knew. Then one day I woke up with a
clearer understanding of reality — I was the rich, and Michael Barnet
with the two dollars in his pocket was the rich. Up until then I had
thought of us as the ordinary people who should not be asked to give
up their chance for the "good life."

"What difference would our small sacrifices make anyway?" If
we are not asking that question ourselves, someone else is. Every day
people tell the mission groups of The Potter's House how foolish is
our vision of a city made new. They are willing to concede that pock-

ets of abscess are being cleared up, and that in isolated places the impossible is happening, but they point to the disease that is erupting in ten other places while this work goes on, and they ask one of those questions that all sound alike: "Why try?" "What's the use?" "What difference will it make?"

Our giving makes a difference in the lives of each of us. Even if we had no responsibility for the creation of our cities and the creation of our world, we would still have the responsibility of continuing the creation of our own lives. Every single act determines our being and shapes the persons we become.

A young friend once told me that a bank cashier had given him ten dollars more than she should have. "I guess," he said, "I was foolish to return it . . . most people wouldn't have." What we do not understand is that our small private acts are supremely important in the creation of our own lives. They determine how we feel about ourselves and how we feel about others. The act of returning money that does not belong to one creates a certain kind of person — the act of keeping it, another. These opposite acts produce very different kinds of people. This is what Kierkegaard is telling us when he warns that in eternity there is no crowd — only the "single one."

Too often we swallow a myth when we believe in our power-lessness. A newspaper columnist once criticized a church for selling ten thousand shares of stock in a company to protest its hiring practices. He contended that the church was advertising her powerlessness. "What are ten thousand shares of stock," he asked, "in a company that has two million outstanding?" In the financial section of that same newspaper, article after article commented on the failure of the United States Government to strengthen the national economy, despite its aggressive and prodding efforts. Cautious buying was cited as a primary reason. According to a spokesperson for Madison Avenue, advertising had to change if it was to reach the new consumer who was showing more interest in corporate integrity when selecting a product. "The winds that are stirring our society are strong ones," he wrote, "and the consumer we face is a new creature — smarter, sensitive to social problems. And much more thoughtful about . . . purchases and their real value." For our own sakes, we must each sell our two shares of stock in structures of oppression, even if ours is a solitary gesture; but the fact is that it will make a difference in the direction a nation takes.

In February, 1982, Justine Merritt went on retreat to pray for guidance for her life. She had a feeling that despite her meaningful activities something was out of focus. Many of her friends were engaged in the peace movement, but she had successfully resisted any involvement. "Don't talk to me about nuclear war," she had said. "I don't want to hear it."

On the retreat she knew that she could no longer maintain her distance from the peace effort. In the following weeks she envisioned a great Ribbon of Peace that would encircle the Pentagon in August 1985, the fortieth anniversary of the bombings of Hiroshima and Nagasaki. She wrote that she saw "The Ribbon as segments of fabric sewn together, with each segment being a symbol of what we cannot bear to think of as lost forever in nuclear war." Justine Merritt embroidered the names of loved ones on a segment of cloth, eighteen by thirty-six inches. She wrote of the experience:

> When I was making my own Ribbon panel, I found that as I would thread my needle, I was confronting the fear, confronting the grief and terror. As I drew the needle up through the cloth, I was praying for peace, and the prayer became an affirmation of life. The very task of creating my panel helped empower me to face the reality of living in a nuclear age.
>
> I faced the reality that the lives of my grandchildren are in jeopardy. Beethoven's melodies are in jeopardy, every shell and flower and bird is in jeopardy, and the planet is as vulnerable as I am. I thought about how many weapons there are, and faced the realization that all this could be lost, not just an apple blossom this spring, but the newest grandchild, who is only six months old. I faced the terror that I might actually survive, that I might "prevail" in such an outrageous act of genocide, and in confronting those realities and turning them into an affirmation of life, I felt less grief-stricken, less afraid, less angry, and more committed than ever to working for peace. In creating my panel for The Ribbon, I felt a great sense of healing . . .[3]

Change takes place when those who are earth-bound have communion with lives that are rooted and grounded in a transcendent order, and they themselves begin to glimpse what they had not seen before. In the company of persons of vision, we do not have the same need to clutch what is ours; we have a greater need to do justice and love mercy.

Someone makes promises about fasting — and we do not argue the theology of it. Tomorrow there will be time to pore over Scripture, listen to our spiritual fathers and mothers, read the health books, and write our own dissertations on fasting, but right now a woman is telling us things of the Spirit and we want to be in on what she is in on.

A man from a pulpit speaks of a people who are undertaking the discipline of fasting, and moving out to say to the oppressed of the world, "We would like to be with you in your struggle, on whatever terms you name," and a few more of us awake from our slumbering and ask to be included.

The promise of prayer is the coming of the springtime of the church, when each of us will know that what we do *does* matter, when we each will take up the task of making a new life and a new world, when we each will know that we do not struggle alone.

PRAYER AND DISCIPLINE

The experience of fasting for one year was a different experience for each one of us in the mission groups. Along the way we encountered obstacles, not the least of which was pride camouflaged in a variety of disguises. In the early months those who experienced no difficulty with the discipline sounded a note of self-satisfaction because they were able to fast with such ease. Others who suffered pangs of hunger and actual weakness every fast day resisted admitting the necessity of having to modify the discipline of total abstinence that most of their friends were maintaining. Fortunately someone put into our hands a paper thought to be from a teaching by St. Francis:

> Each of you should have regard for his own nature. Though this or that one may be able to sustain himself on less food than someone else, still I will not have one who needs more food try to imitate the former in that. Taking his own nature into consideration, let him bestow on his body what it needs in order to be able to serve the spirit. Just as we are bound to avoid superfluity in eating, for it harms body and soul, so must we be beware of excessive abstaining, yes even more so, because the Lord wants mercy and not sacrifice.

Equally helpful was the story of the brother who, overzealous in fasting, one night roused the community with loud cries that he was starving. Lest embarrassment be added to his anguish, St. Francis had all the brothers get up and eat a meal with him.

Many of us in the mission groups discovered how very social is the act of eating, which is probably why the short Gospel accounts give so much space to food — outdoor picnics, a supper behind closed doors, a fish fry at dawn beside the Sea of Tiberias. We did not miss the food as much as we missed the communion of breaking bread with another person. Slowly, ever so slowly, we began to know the mysterious collaboration between body and spirit, and to learn that the appetite for food and the desire for the company of a friend could be transmuted into communion with Jesus Christ and the breaking of bread with him in the communion supper. We learned in our fasting the meaning of the Scripture that had been familiar to some of us from childhood: "Here I stand knocking at the door; if anyone hears my voice and opens the door, I will come in and sit down to supper with him and he with me" (Rev. 3:20, *NEB*).

We received two anonymous reports from those days of fasting. One was entitled *Steps on a Journey*:

> 1. I felt it a great accomplishment to go a whole day without food. Congratulated myself on the fact that I found it so easy. Also, enjoyed the fact that I lost weight and could indulge more freely in sweets.
>
> 2. Began to see that the above was hardly the goal of fasting. Was helped in this by beginning to feel hunger. Also, hated to forego the social aspects of food.
>
> 3. Still could put food out of my mind with a large degree of grace. Began to relate the food fast to other areas of my life where I was more compulsive. Always thought I had to have eight hours' sleep each night. I could see this was not essential. My world was not going to fall apart if I did not have my usual quota of sleep any more than it would if I did not have my usual quota of meals. Began to move out of the grip of necessity in other areas. I did not have to have a seat on the bus to be contented, or to be cool in the summer and warm when it was cold.
>
> 4. Continued to feel less at the mercy of my own desires — more detached. I was still picking the easiest day on which to fast — the one on which I would experience the least denial — would have the least

reminders of food. Despite this, began to be hungrier. No day seemed like a good day for fasting. Reflected more on Christ's suffering and the suffering of those who are hungry and have hungry babies. Discovered with my friends that I could suffer a little hunger in order that others could suffer a little less hunger.

5. Six months after beginning the fast discipline, I began to see why a two-year period had been suggested. The experience changes along the way. Hunger on fast days became acute, and the temptation to eat stronger. For the first time I was using the day to find God's will for my life. Began to think about what it meant to surrender one's life.

6. I now know that prayer and fasting must be intricately bound together. There is no other way, and yet that way is not yet combined in me. This is where I am at this writing.

The other report was entitled *Personal Reflections on Fasting:*

My initial effort of fasting this particular year has had special meaning and provided new insight for me. It has pointed up for me with new clarity just how strong I am — but I really mean how weak my strength is — when dependent on my own resources. I learned how quickly I had to resort to God's strength — how soon my own energy, my own joyfulness, my own high spirits were depleted. All too soon I felt physically weak, emotionally depressed, an angry man! I learned again to be thankful to God for his gifts to me and my family, and I gained new insight into the angry mood of the hungry!! I felt vicarious suffering as I prolonged the fast, tried to live into the skin of the ghetto poor — just tried being hungry with the poor. But I learned too in my most suffering moments, when I turned to God and prayed for others, his strength flowed to me and I quickly forgot my own physical feelings — and I knew God's strength and resources were available not only to me but to all who asked.

These were not easy lessons, it took three weeks of false starts for me to get with it — three weeks of guilt and remorse, too quickly rationalizing my sinfulness and weakness and giving excuses — because food was there for the eating. And I was not deprived as those who had no food within arm's reach or a human friend to provide. I felt again humility and my weak humanness. I felt that sackcloth and ashes would have been proper dress in my weakness. But the lesson was there and the insight comes inspired by my communion with God.

As we had agreed, at the end of a year fasting was dropped as a discipline of The Potter's House mission groups. The only group that kept it as a corporate discipline was the one that had argued against it in the second month and had wanted all the groups to call off the whole idea. In the other mission groups we were once again on our own. No one held us accountable for the discipline; nor did anyone offer encouragement. Unless we asked, we did not know whether a person was fasting.

On those few occasions when we identified ourselves and compared notes, we found that our experience was the same in a number of respects. The fasting discipline became extraordinarily difficult to keep after it was dropped as a group discipline. Even those who had had no doubts about continuing went through a period of not being able to stay with it. Those who gave it up light-heartedly discovered months later that it was a discipline they wanted in their lives. A few would fast one week and not the next, depending on how socially convenient it was. The half dozen people I knew who, at that time at least, continued with the discipline found it necessary to integrate their lives once again around the decision. This time the struggle was an interior one — all the arguments we had to overcome were arguments in ourselves.

Whatever our private decision, we were each more aware that there was only one important movement required of us as a fast. Isaiah had penned it long ago:

> Is not this what I require of you as a fast:
>   to loose the fetters of injustice
>   to untie the knots of the yoke,
>   to snap every yoke
>   and set free those who have been crushed?
>
> - - - - - -
>
> Then, if you call, the Lord will answer;
>   if you cry to him, he will say, "Here I am."
>   —Isaiah 58:6, 9, *NEB*

Each of the mission groups that staff The Potter's House has had to struggle to find its own way to be involved in the creation of a new city. No group moves easily into the next phase of its life. Anyone who takes seriously a vision has to do battle with opposing forces in the world, but the only battles of any significance are those we fight within our own lives. To be in earnest about a vision is to think about strategy — how to take what is out in the distance and bring it into the here and now where it can be perceived by ordinary sight. Whenever we struggle with that question, our understanding of the cost grows until a far more exacting question confronts us: "Am I willing to pay that cost?" And once again another person is led by the Spirit into the wilderness. Dangled before us are all the satisfactions and rewards that will come simply by keeping on with our lives as they are. All that belongs to one level of understanding in us makes war on the light which has broken through from a higher level.

In the temptation story is the vivid account of that conflict in Christ. It is a conflict between two orders — heaven and earth — which must rage within every person if there is to be a new age of the Spirit. The choice each of us makes — how that conflict is resolved in us — determines whether or not ministering angels come, whether we walk under the sign of the Cross. What is true for the individual is true for the group.

PRAYER AND POLITICS

While other mission groups worked in the areas of housing, programs for the elderly, and schools for tutoring the young, the Thursday night mission group began to wrestle with the problem of how to confront and change those structures and systems in the city that were destroying the very people they were set up to serve. How does the church become a servant people in the area of politics? How does it combine in its own life politics and prayer?

The Thursday mission group's initial strategy was to form relationships with the twenty-five members of the House District Committee who were influential in determining policy and legislation for the voteless District of Columbia. Members of the Thursday group also chose two or three Congressional representatives with whom they would establish a special and unique relationship. They would pray for those people and try to attain some understanding in depth of the issues before them. Eventually, it was hoped, contacts would be made with individuals and organizations in the home constituency of the selected Congressional members.

Often the stand of a public representative was the opposite of the one that we ourselves so fervently took. When this was the situation, we dealt in prayer with our own feelings until we could respond by caring, regardless of how damaging to the mind and soul of a nation we appraised a given course of action to be. As a mission group, we struggled with our hostile responses by trying to live into the world of the representatives we had chosen. We tried to appreciate the pressures and influences that play on the life of a public figure. We tried to see that person not as a power symbol who is the enemy of our hope, but as a person striving, however mistakenly, for what we all want and need — love and acceptance and belonging.

Our plan was for each mission group, when it had a more informed heart and mind, to seek to bring into being fifty or sixty mission groups, each having not fewer than five and not more than twelve members. These groups would then relate to significant committees of the Senate or the House, studying the areas of responsibility, agenda and functioning of that selected committee. In addition, each group would take on about ten members of Congress or the Senate in the intimate way already described. Our goal was to have every member of the House, Senate, and important committees covered by some mission group. We hoped to learn what it meant to hold our representatives in prayer. We agreed that, when it was appropriate, we would write letters, send telegrams, and lobby in any way that might be effective. And we covenanted that, if ever we were so bold as to believe that we had a prophetic word (which is to say a word that could heal), we would trust our perseverance and strength of limb to carry us to the place where it was to be spoken.

PRAYER AND CONTEMPLATION

In The Potter's House we struggled to balance our study of the problems of the city with our study of the teachings of the masters of prayer. In many ways the coffee house was an ideal laboratory for different kinds of prayer. When we were reading Kelly's *The Gathered Meeting,* the assignment was to come to grips with the meaning of serious preparation preceding worship. The months we studied

Brother Lawrence's *Practice of the Presence of God,* we endeavored in a new way to do the work of a coffee house evening in awareness of and by a conscious turning to God. We might have guests waiting for their orders to be taken, tables to clear, and questions being thrown at us, but Brother Lawrence had assured us his situation was not much different. "The time of business," he said, "does not with me differ from the time of prayer, and in the noise and clatter of my kitchen, while several persons are at the same time calling for different things, I possess God in as great tranquillity as if I were upon my knees at the Blessed Sacrament."[4]

One of our members was appointed to walk on the half hour among the tables, lightly ringing a small bell to remind us of our exercise of the Presence of God. I wish that I could report that we, like Brother Lawrence, reached that state of which he wrote: *"It would be as difficult for me not to think of God as it was at first to accustom myself to it."*[5] Then the world could come and have conversations with us on the practice of the Presence of God. As it is, the world will do better to read Brother Lawrence.

After Brother Lawrence, we went through a period of struggling anew with the meaning of silence. Our special guide was Geoffrey Hoyland, whose little pamphlet, *The Use of Silence,*[6] we returned to again and again in our journeying. For a time we held many of our meetings in silence. Some of The Potter's House groups worked in quiet the whole night, speaking only with customers. Others set aside an hour in the evening to keep a wordless communion.

All these efforts were preparation for our reading of the mystics — or contemplatives as I prefer to call them because the word has a more earthy sound. In looking back it seems to me that the time we were seriously considering the meaning of contemplation for our lives coincided with the time when we all unawares took a special fall from grace. Subtly, almost stealthily, when we were absorbed in the adventure of prayer, the lapse occurred.

We had practiced recollection and the use of silence and felt prepared to develop the art of meditation. We had firmly in mind the instructions of the books we had read on this subject. When we came together for our evening meeting, we meditated corporately for half an hour on the Scriptures we had pondered during the week. Then we shared the Word that came alive in us, and sometimes as we spoke the Holy Spirit came, and light broke, and we saw what we had not seen — a whole new throbbing universe swung into view — and in us were little movements toward love and freedom. We were excited about Scripture and excited about our times together. For several weeks it seemed as though we moved in a new realm of creativity and joy — and then it all came to an abrupt end, as if a signal had been given and we had obediently returned to a former state.

Shortly thereafter many of us went out and bought good commentaries on Matthew, the Gospel we were currently reading. The unusual thing about this was that we had previously agreed not to use commentaries, but to write our own. Soon less and less of our time together was spent in meditation. The insights on Scripture that we shared came from books. They were good insights, but they were the fruits of someone else's meditation, and no fire burned in us, no new order of existence came into view, no luminous moments of discovery lifted us out of the ordinary.

Reflection on those days reveals a number of factors that might account for our stumbling "at noonday as if it were twilight."[7] To begin with, those who were eager to move into serious meditation had persuaded those who were not so eager to come along. This procedure didn't work out. It never works out. The contemplative way is not a way that can be traveled to please one's friends or to keep them company. St. John of the Cross wrote that God has a different path for every soul. All of our experience affirms his word, but we are slow to absorb what we do not want to learn. Perhaps our own unsureness makes us eager to have companions on the way, or we may fear that our relationships with significant people in our lives will not be as strong if they do not share experiences that are important to us.

In one sense, preparation for contemplative prayer grows out of an awareness of one's aloneness — a feeling of solitude, a knowing that the treasure one is seeking will not be found on any well-trod streets, a willingness to go in search of it alone. Once there, one begins to recognize those who are on the same path, or, in the words of Petru Dumitriu, those whose souls are "filled with intimations of the secret." Dumitriu used the vehicle of a novel to say that we need not even be in a hurry to pass the secret on. "The person aflame with awareness and desire who is already on the edge of the secret will know how to find us, and he will not need any lengthy exposition. A single word will be enough to enlighten him, a single action, a gesture, a look, a smile, a silence . . ."[8]

Another reason for our stumbling was that we had moved too fast and, goaded by the impatient ones, had gone on to new lessons without having mastered old ones. Some felt they were making no progress in their meditation and were bound to derive more benefits from a commentary; others, flushed with success and enthusiastic by nature, kept extending their private times of meditation until something in them rebelled against the whole idea, and they abandoned the pursuit altogether.

Still another factor playing on us was a growing understanding of the implications of the way of prayer that we were following. It is one thing to set aside an hour each day for prayer. It is another to begin to see that what happens in that hour is determined by what we do in the other twenty-three hours. We began to receive hints that prayer was a way of life, and that the claim on "our time" was greater than we had thought. Perhaps Christ had meant that each of us was to keep our own life a house of prayer.

In T.S. Eliot's poem, *The Cocktail Party*, the psychiatrist — or guardian angel — says to Celia:

> If that is what you wish,
> I can reconcile you to the human condition,
> The condition to which some who have gone as far as you
> Have succeeded in returning. They may remember
> The vision they have had, but they cease to regret it . . .[9]

The writer of Hebrews said the same choice was given to those who had a vision of another land: "If their hearts had been in the country they had left, they could have found opportunity to return" (Heb. 11:15, *NEB*). The tenderness, mercy, comfort of God is in that Scripture. God does not uproot, or persuade, or insist, or threaten, nor does God leave us in our anxiety. Instead we are given the opportunity to return, to reconsider the whole adventure and decide whether or not where we are is where we want to be.

My reading of Scripture and the contemplatives, however, makes me believe that this "going back" is possible only for beginners. The mystics are all careful to say that there is a place of no safe return. Once there, we will see what we cannot forget; we will be given knowledge that will cause us suffering if it is not used; a change will happen in us that will be irreversible. If we fall away then, we fall into despair. Christmas Humphreys said it this way: "When once the

inner eye is opened it can never again be closed." As a poet wrote
on reaching this experience:

> "The future lies unmoulded in my hands.
>   A Path winds out before.
> There is no backward way. Behind me stands
>   a closed door."[10]

No one issued more solemn warning than the fourteenth-century
author of *The Cloud of Unknowing* whose prologue to his book on
contemplation begins:

> I charge you and beg you, with all the strength and
> power that love can bring to bear, that whoever you
> may be who possess this book (perhaps you own it, or
> are keeping it, carrying it, or borrowing it) you should,
> quite freely and of set purpose, neither read, write, or
> mention it to anyone, nor allow it to be read, written,
> or mentioned by anyone unless that person is in your
> judgment really and wholly determined to follow
> Christ perfectly. And to follow him not only in the
> active life, but to the utmost height of the contempla-
> tive life that is possible for a perfect soul in a mortal
> body to attain by the grace of God.[11]

The author of *The Cloud* thought it was useless to tell people about
contemplative prayer who were not ready for it. He was convinced
that this book would have no meaning for them. Despite the plea in
its prologue, *The Cloud* is one of the most read and loved of all devotional classics. Rather than the curious, into whose hands the author
was afraid the book might fall, it is much more likely that its readers
have been men and women who dared to think that their urgings to
share in the deep things of the spirit qualified them to read on.

Despite our wavering and stumbling, despite the division within
us and the differences in understanding that we had (and still have),
the mission groups of The Potter's House began to define themselves
as people in the process of becoming contemplatives. Our journeying
with Meister Eckhart, Brother Lawrence, E. Herman, Romano Guardini, Dag Hammarskjöld, and others had fanned the smoldering
urgings in us and created a hunger for God deeper than we had
known before. We had traveled in the company of the saints long
enough to be aware of the possibilities for life and freedom that come

to those who are willing to cultivate an inner solitude, which is the large task of the contemplative way. We had approached the place of conflict, or decision, or death.

In the Old Testament whenever a person reached a critical crossroad in life or had an encounter with the Living God, that person gave a name to that place, thus securing the memory of a numinous event. I would like to name this juncture in our lives "The Place of Death," for it is here where we had to decide between going on or going back, and each choice involved a dying to something.

To go on toward the light that we see is to die to the old. This dying is a real death — a dead, dead death. When it is over there is no going back. To try is to walk through a ghost town where nothing lives. Where we look for meaning, we find none; we ourselves fall into meaninglessness. The message of Scripture is clear: "No one who puts his hand to the plow and looks back is fit for the kingdom of God" (Luke 9:62, *RSV*).

And yet to choose to return to the old while there is still time — before we have looked fully on the new — is to die to all the possibilities that belong to the life which is rooted and grounded in the Eternal — "from him who has not, even what he has will be taken away" (Matt. 25:29, *RSV*). To make this choice, however, is to be disturbed no longer by intimations that something is out of joint with one's life.

In either way there is a death, but in each way there is also a peace. To have one's total being unified around a decision is to put an end to conflict. If we have an undivided heart, we walk our path with gladness, leaving others free to find their path. We are most defensive and threatened when we are uncertain about our choice. Some ridicule the "good" life because it attracts them more than they want to admit; others, for the same reason, brush aside the contemplative life as the way of a few mystical church types whose feet are not on the ground. Somewhere in most of us is a small voice that cannot say "no" to the contemplative way, and in us deep away stirs the uneasy feeling that we are missing out on what really is important.

Any reading of the contemplatives will confirm our fears. These travelers warn us not to begin on this inward adventure without the strong promptings of the Spirit, but they believe that an inner quickening of life happens as one wills to take time to tend the small seed in one's self which harbors the faith that there is infinitely more than we can now see or understand. That seed can die, or it can grow and shoot forth branches. When the mystics speak of prayer, they are talking about that which will create in us a new structure of consciousness. From this there is no turning back.

Prayer brings about a fundamental change in the quality of a person's being, so that life is lived on an entirely different level of existence. Mysterious as this may sound, it actually has to do with changes in very ordinary aspects of living, such as increased awareness of what we see and hear, a heightened degree of receptivity, a growing capacity to respond — to be engaged in the moment as one who is fully present. Because the way to the place of quiet in one's self has been learned, one is able to live out of that center, and to penetrate the mystery that lies everywhere around.

In his book, *The Master Game,* Robert S. de Ropp cites the myth of the king who went mad and moved to the cellar of his palace. There he sat in the midst of rags and bones and worthless things which he clung to as treasures. His ministers would urge him to leave, reminding him of all the rooms in the palace above crowded with real treasures, but the king was never impressed by the splendors they recounted. He insisted that he was living in the rooms they were describing. "His illusion," declares de Ropp, "was such that he saw the wretched cellar as a palace and the rags and bones that he had collected as precious jewels."[12]

This same theme is found in the writings of the mystics. Like the king's ministers, these adventurers are striving to awaken us to the fact that there are glorious unknown rooms in our own individual houses, and that the key to unlocking the doors of those rooms and coming upon the treasure to be found there is contemplative prayer.

The mystics never report that they are traveling a spiral way meant for the privileged few. They write extensively of their journeying to encourage others because they feel that it is possible for any person to experience the reality of God. More than this, they declare that a deepening life of prayer is essential for wholeness and an expanding consciousness of God and self. They insist that contemplative prayer is a natural human activity that requires not special gifts or powers, but rather the training of those latent faculties that every person has which, when developed, will open new doors in every area of life.

In the mission groups of The Potter's House the "yes" we have said, however falteringly, to the contemplative life is what makes sense of our covenant — a covenant which is perplexing to so many. We have agreed with one another to set aside an hour each day for recollection, meditative reading, prayer, and the keeping of a journal in which we reflect on the inner and outer events of our lives. As alien as it may sound to modern ears, we are not ashamed to say that we are striving to be apprentices in the art of contemplative prayer. Those who seek membership in the mission groups of The Potter's House must be eager to embrace this way. They must earnestly want to be part of a community whose covenent will sustain and support them by holding them accountable not only for the disciplines of the inward journey, but also for those of the outward journey — the disciplines which help us to see our crucified Lord in the institutions and streets and "holy places" of a nation, and enable us to be a part of the Resurrection story in our land.

Contrary to the commonly held image, the mystics are men and women of action. Meister Eckhart said, "Even if a man were in rapture like St. Paul and knew of a man who was in need of food he would do better by feeding him than by remaining in ecstasy."[13] Out of the literature of prayer, Christmas Humphreys passes on to us this counsel: "Unless each step in inner growth finds corresponding expression in service to mankind the student treads a dangerous path, and works in vain."[14]

In the coffee house we responded to this counsel. If we had to choose in any given moment between prayer and joining in the struggle of the hungry poor, we would turn from our praying. This is why I write of prayer within a community of persons who search to find their part in the movement for liberation by the oppressed of the world. Also, I feel more comfortable writing about the life of prayer in a coffee house than I would writing about prayer in the abstract. Too often we treat prayer as removed from the context of our lives, an activity that ordinary people raising families and following professions must be content to leave to monastic orders or to women's prayer groups. That attitude belongs to an outmoded society. Though it is true that few church leaders today give serious consideration to prayer or silence, to conclude that the currents of the age are moving against the contemplative life could well be a misreading of the signs. We may be on the verge of an era in which there will develop a whole new sensitivity to the realm of the Spirit.

According to Freud, when new factors are being raised into our consciousness, the first reaction is resistance — sometimes open denial. In all the segments of society today we find resistance, manifested not only in the rejection of the old, but in strong opposition to the new which is impinging on us and threatening the life style we have known. This makes for some of the fire in the world today — fire that can rage out of control and destroy us, or purify and transform. Marie-Louise von Franz says that "the fire is really the great judge and determines the difference between the corruptible and the incorruptible, between what is relevant and what is irrelevant."[15]Without fire nothing happens. "But because you are lukewarm, neither hot nor cold, I will spit you out of my mouth" (Rev. 3:16, *NEB*).

No calm is on the scene today. No tepid waters flow within or around us. The anguish we know and the tensions that tear at our lives and tear at the fabric of the church and every other existing institution have the potential of readying us for a new epoch when there will be fresh manifestations of the Spirit. Perhaps we shall be able to take our fire — our passion — and beat with it upon the Cloud of Unknowing which is between us and God. That dark cloud, say the saints, can be penetrated by love. The one who breaks through it knows unutterable joy — a new tomorrow.

If we believe this, believe that God can be known, that we do not have to base our belief on someone else's experience, then we can have some confidence that we are ready for the work of contemplation. The urge to this kind of prayer is fueled by the knowledge that God can be "caught and held," and that we can know a unity and power within as well as an "at-oneness" with the whole created order. Without some small spark of that conviction, we lack the energy and motivation essential for the inner work of prayer. In his introduction to *The Cloud,* Clifton Wolters notes that, in the seventy-five short chapters of the book, the word "grace" and its cognates are found over ninety times, and that there are, in addition, many other references to the providential, prevenient work of God.[16] Nonetheless, *The Cloud* stresses, as does every other great writing on prayer, the difficulty of the way. Toil, work, labor, and striving are important words in the vocabulary of the saints and punctuate the guides they have given to us. "Waiting upon God is not idleness," said St. Bernard, "but work which beats all other work to one unskilled in it."[17]

Perhaps the hardness of the way helps us to discern that another sign of one's readiness to embark on the work of prayer is a certain discontent, coupled with an abandonment of the search for answers outside one's own life. Part of the law of compensation may be that people with dis-ease force open the locked doors of their inner palaces in a way that people of placid temperament and stable emotions are rarely impelled to do. "Dis-eased" people seem equipped by their unrest for the exacting road of the saints. They may struggle as much with the disciplines as the next person, fail as often, but the imperative to keep trying burns deep in them and sustains their efforts.

Another mark of contemplative persons is a passionate interest in their own liberation. If we are serious about deepening our prayer life, we must have some understanding of what binds us — have wrestled with the darkness within us — and then with the angel for his blessing. We cannot, with safety, by-pass our sufferings. Until we have struggled to acknowledge and understand our fears or those vague uneasy feelings, we have not done the preliminary work that is essential for prayer at the level described by the contemplatives.

If we have yet to do that work, if we do not know in our beings any holy discontent, if there is no longing in us toward God, we need not draw the conclusion either that we are not meant to be contemplatives, or that we lack the temperament or capacity for apprenticeship. A safer assumption is that we have not yet had experiences which have awakened us and stirred our longing. As fundamental a step as we can take in this direction is learning to meditate on Scripture — learning first to hear God's word, to let it inform and take root in us. This may be extremely difficult, for the churches have no courses on meditation, despite the fact that it is an art that must be learned from those who have mastered it, and despite the fact that the supreme task of the church is to listen to the Word of God. No other group has that assignment. Other groups are engaged in various forms of mission, but only the church is committed to hearing the Word of God and proclaiming it to our age.

For the Christian the channel which is at the heart of listening is Scripture. To take a book of the Bible, to immerse one's self in it and to be grasped by it, is to have one's life literally revolutionized. This requires study and the training of attention. The student stays with it through barren day after barren day, until at last the meaning is clear, and transformation happens.

In his biography of Dietrich Bonhoeffer, Eberhard Bethge quotes this passage from a letter that Bonhoeffer wrote to his brother, Karl-Friedrich:

I think I am right in saying that I would only achieve true inward clarity and sincerity by really starting work on the Sermon on the Mount. Here alone lies the force that can blow all this stuff and nonsense sky-high, in a fireworks display that will leave nothing behind but one or two charred remains. The restoration of the Church must surely depend on a new kind of monasticism, having nothing in common with the old but a life of uncompromising adherence to the Sermon on the Mount in imitation of Christ. I believe the time has come to rally men together for this.[18]

When Bonhoeffer began the seminary at Finkenwalde, out of which community came *Life Together,* he included in the morning schedule of the seminarians half an hour's silent meditation on the Scripture which they had corporately agreed on. Bethge reports that the assignment was perplexing to the young men, none of whom understood it. Resentment and rebellion smoldered in the community. "But not at once," wrote Bethge, "for on the one hand the ordinands felt entitled to spend the half-hour as they themselves saw fit, and on the other they were put to shame by their director's evident ability to concentrate upon this exercise."[19] On one occasion when Bonhoeffer had to be away for two weeks, the exercise was abandoned altogether. He had left the House in charge of his assistant, W. Rott, who had understood Bonhoeffer's conception of meditation no better than the students, and was therefore unable to enforce the exercise.

When Bonhoeffer returned and learned that the morning exercise had been abandoned, he set aside an evening for the students to ventilate their feelings, but he had no intention of submitting the matter of meditation to a majority decision. It was understood from the beginning that the exercises were to be continued. As time went by, few of the ordinands tried to evade keeping the discipline and many continued the practice in those crucial years after the seminary was dissolved. Until his arrest Bonhoeffer remained a faithful director of souls, and in a circular letter to former students gave them weekly selections from Scripture for meditation, sometimes with the exhortation not to abandon the practice. These exercises were later to be of immeasurable help not only to the young men, many of whom were drafted into Hitler's army, but to Bonhoeffer himself. "In 1943 and 1944," wrote Bethge, "when he was compelled to lead a cruelly lonely existence, the exercises he had practiced at Finkenwalde proved an invaluable solace."[20]

Another preparation for the contemplative life is simply to be in the company of contemplatives — even if it be only through living with their writings. In actuality, however, the church can be a community of contemplatives, if we can give a fresh impetus to the interpretation of that word. Its meaning may be contained in that short Scripture, "Jesus called twelve to be with him" (Mark 3:14, *RSV*). Is not the call to contemplation simply the call to be with Jesus?

There is a story about a man who went each day to sit in the dark of a church. One day as he came out, a perplexed friend inquired what he did during the long time he spent inside the church. "I just look at God," he answered, "and God looks at me." That is the call to contemplation — a call to looking. Out of that looking flows an amazing activity which is different from normal activity. It is action that flows out of the Resurrection power. With it comes a peculiar effectiveness — a strange kind of congruence, a flowing together. Events happen and events fit together, and are accepted and understood at another level because the action comes out of a relationship.

Clifton Wolters sums it all up in a few lines:

> Contemplation is not the pleasant reaction to a celestial sunset, nor is it the perpetual twitter of heavenly birdsong. It is not even an emotion. It is the awareness of God, known and loved at the core of one's being.[21]

The exercises in the following section are ones that we use in the mission groups of The Potter's House. We struggle with them, rebel against them, lapse away from, and return to them. They were adapted from exercises given by Evelyn Underhill in her small volume entitled *Practical Mysticism*.[22] The practice of them will not make a contemplative of any one in a few weeks, but used in conjunction with the readings, the exercises will help us learn to meditate and to understand better the way of the contemplative. If we practice consistently over a long time, our experience of both our inner and outer world will be intensified. Not all at once, but eventually we will find doors opening that lead us deep into the ground of our own being — that central place of stillness where God speaks and we understand for ourselves the meaning of the divine-human birth.

The exercises are arduous because they conflict with the style of life we have known and the demand for instant results which our culture fosters in us. They require us to do violence to other drives and habitual ways of responding. Jesus said that the violent take the kingdom (Matt. 11:12). Revolutionary acts are necessary to effect a real revolution in the outer order; for the church, revolution means a change in consciousness — a whole new way of hearing and perceiving, an unleashing of the winds of revival, a flowing of living water.

If no doors open for you, your efforts will not have been wasted. You will have gained a mastery over your attention that will serve you well whatever is the way of your climbing. Others are traveling toward the same goal along different paths. We must find the way that is uniquely ours. One word of caution: if we seek our own liberation — if the high call of God in Christ is to be free persons — though there are different ways to move toward that goal, not one of them is easy.

We can choose a different way. We cannot find an easy way.

All roads that lead to becoming our real selves will require us to sell all that we have. The Kingdom is always at hand, always available to us, but we must be totally surrendered to the adventure. Nothing may have a place of more importance than the search — not wife, or husband, or children, or property.

In The Potter's House we struggle with the rules, struggle with our own indifference, procrastination, or inclination to leave praise of God to spring days and music festivals — struggle with the temptations of unbelief, discouragement, upsurge of old desires. We fall, and get up, and start out again.

We continue to struggle for our own liberation and the liberation of the city around us. In our city small bands of children roam the streets until midnight. For diversion they pound on the doors of The Potter's House and shove through its mail box odd pieces of junk, part of their day's loot. Above those same streets the old are hidden away in bare and dirty rooms. "The bad thing about being old," said one aged person, "is that no one ever touches you."

From the young and old of our city we have learned that America does not treat well her poor and helpless. The poverty of experience that we see in our ghettos is compounded in the public institutions of our land where young and old, the mentally ill, the retarded, and physically handicapped clamor for normal stimulation and human touching, and where still others have moved beyond yearning to apathy, despair, mindless shrieks and moans.

We believe that this can change and that we can have a part in the coming of a new age for us all. We believe with Bonhoeffer that the restoration of the church depends on a new kind of monasticism — the putting of the Sermon on the Mount into our own lives and living out our vision of what the Sermon means in spheres of politics, education, medicine, housing, and all those concrete situations where we find ourselves. We want to be in the company of those who rally people together for this.

EXERCISE 3:

The Practice of Silence

Practice for five minutes each day, preferably on arising, the withdrawing of your attention from all outward and inward consideration, and, by will, concentrate your attention within yourself. When scattered thoughts or words intrude, with deliberation cut them off, and push steadfastly toward the silence — your own center. This is called in the literature of prayer "a gathering in," or being present to one's deeper self. Learn what this means.

When you are able consistently to practice the five minutes of recollection in the morning, add another five-minute period at night, and then eventually add still another in the middle of the day. If you will persevere with this exercise, you will learn to walk the path to the quiet place in yourself even in the midst of activities, or when you note that your feelings run too strong, or when you are up against the tumultuous feelings of others. Too often our point of gravity is outside ourselves in events or other people, or at the circumference of our lives. This is a state of lostness. This exercise of focusing your attention will help you to find your own center, and then to act and speak out of that place of quiet.

Another helpful exercise in training attention, which can be used with the above one, is to practice being present during the day to whatever you undertake. A way to do this is to ask for the Holy Spirit, and to say something like, "This half-hour I commit myself to the task of letter writing," or "This hour I commit myself to being present to the person who has come to see me," or "Until their bedtime I commit myself to playing with my children and to listening to them."

Distractions and demands have a way of scattering us, so that it is not uncommon to be doing one thing and thinking of another. We are not wholly present to what is at hand and, if we live most of the hours of the day like this, the pattern will follow us into the time of prayer. If we practice being present to each task during the day, then we will be more able to be present at the time of prayer and not be distracted by thoughts that would otherwise claim our attention.

In the same way, if we can learn to quiet our thoughts at the time of prayer and to be, as it were, present to ourselves, such training of our attention will enable us to be fully present to the claims upon us in other hours. This is one of the reasons why persons who pray will tell you that prayer saves time and enables them to accomplish more than they would ordinarily be able to do. More than this, prayer allows us to live in the "now-moment," which means that we are fully involved — seeing, hearing and experiencing life as it is given. The content of the moment, therefore, gives content to our lives. We are changed by it. Meister Eckhart writes

> "God is a simple presence, a stay-at-home in himself.
> With any creature, as regards her noble nature, the
> more she sits at home the more of herself she gives
> out."[1]

In the beginning it will be very difficult for you to stay at home in your innermost self. You will fly out to all kinds of thoughts — the dishes in the sink, the unanswered mail, a neglected person, the money you have invested — there will be no end to the thoughts that you have. One way of settling down is to say before you ever begin, "I know many worthy things will claim my attention, but I have reserved this time to root my life in another order of Reality so that I can move into a whole new consciousness and be open in a new way to the whole of life." If this does not help you to quiet your thoughts, then search for a way that does. What is helpful to one person may not be helpful to another. At first — regardless of the method you use

— it will be difficult to stay at home in yourself even during the period you have set aside for prayer. In time, however, you will find it possible to "center-in" even in the midst of activity.

Each day read meditatively one or two of the writings given in the following section. They have been selected to help with the exercises — to give encouragement and instruction. If you find one especially helpful, read it often. *But do not read in place of practicing.*

NOTES ON POSTURE

All the masters of prayer put great emphasis on posture. Body, mind and spirit cannot be separated. The outward attitude of the body will determine in part the inner attitude of prayer. This is why the East with its emphasis on meditation puts a corresponding emphasis on the disciplines of the body. Our body is not unrelated to our prayer life. We pray with the whole of ourselves. Prayer is concerned with unifying the conflicting elements within us, but essential to this unification is the practice of disciplines which attend to the union between spirit and body, so that the outward form of prayer is related to the inward form. This togetherness of all our parts is essential to moving toward union with God — an at-oneness with life. Msgr. Romano Guardini, in emphasizing that the proper outward manner helps to nurture the inner attitude of prayer, points out that the simple Christian act of kneeling is intended as a "posture of discipline, not of comfort."[2]

Hatha Yoga exercises can be helpful preparation for recollection and the other exercises in prayer which follow. A simpler means of preparing for recollection is to sit in a straight chair, feet on the floor, hands on the knees, the back straight and bent slightly forward, so that the spine comfortably supports itself. Holding this position, one gives attention to the sensing and relaxing of one's whole body, beginning with the toes and ending with the different parts of the face — eyes, mouth, ears, eyebrows.

A helpful article appeared some time ago in *Main Currents in Modern Thought* entitled "Meditation for School Children," in which the author, Dr. M. Lietaert Peerbolte, recommended that some form of meditation be made a part of the educational curriculum, "even if it be only quiet self-recollection." Dr. Peerbolte, who has been a practicing psychiatrist and psychoanalyst in The Hague, Holland, since 1935, stressed the importance of bodily relaxation in achieving an inner silence. He suggested the following simple exercises. These take only a few minutes and can easily be practiced during the day as help in attaining a meditative attitude toward life — a heightened sense of "at-one-ness with daily life experiences, with one's work, and one's milieu."

1. Sit in a comfortable chair, if possible an armchair.
2. Place both feet on the ground, with arms extended along armrests.
3. Sit easily and quietly.
4. After doing this very simple and agreeable exercise for a few minutes, e.g., twice a day for two days, start concentrating on the right arm during the exercise (left-handed people should concentrate on the left arm). Ask yourself whether this arm is quite at rest. Generally it will be observed that there are some muscle-tensions and contractions in the arm, even when one tries to deepen the feelings of rest.
5. After practicing this exercise for a fortnight or so, twice a day for from one to five minutes, you will observe a feeling of lassitude and heaviness in the arm. This is the indicator of the arm's relaxation. During this fortnight of exercise, however, one must avoid every willful effort to provoke the feeling of heaviness.

The aim of these simple exercises is bodily relaxation as preparation for the development of a relaxed mental attitude.[3]

ATTAINING COLLECTEDNESS

The mysterious place into which you must step if you want to get hold of yourself does exist. Take the step and you will know it. It is not merely a place, it is a centre of power; it is something quite distinct from that realm of your being which is constantly changing, fleeting, and dissolving. It is substantial and everlasting. It is you; your "self," your proper being. From "there" and through it you can still your unrest. There you can take root and be present; from there you can gather in all that is dispersed; lift the weight off your mind and lighten your darkness.

Prayer must begin with this collectedness. As said before, it is not easy. How little of it we normally possess becomes painfully clear as soon as we make the first attempt. When we try to compose ourselves, unrest redoubles in intensity, not unlike the manner in which at night, when we try to sleep, cares or desires assail us with a force they do not possess during the day. When we want to be truly "present" we feel how powerful are the voices trying to call us away. As soon as we try to be unified and to obtain mastery over ourselves, we experience the full impact and meaning of distraction. And when we try to be awake and receptive to the holy object, we are seized by an inertness which lowers our spirit. All this is inevitable; we must endure it and persevere; otherwise we shall never learn to pray.

Everything depends on this state of collectedness. No effort to obtain it is ever wasted. And even if the whole duration of our prayer should be applied to this end only, the time thus used would have been well employed. For collectedness itself is prayer. In times of distress, illness or great exhaustion, it can be most beneficial to content oneself with such a "prayer of collectedness." It will calm, fortify and help. Finally, if at first we achieve no more than the understanding of how much we lack in inner unity, something will have been gained, for in some way we would have made contact with that centre which knows no distraction.

Romano Guardini
Prayer in Practice (pp. 20-21)

DISCERNING INNER MEANING

Words in a poem, sounds in movement, rhythm in space, attempt to recapture personal meaning in personal time and space from out of the sights and sounds of a depersonalized, dehumanized world. They are bridgeheads into alien territory. They are acts of insurrection. Their source is from the Silence at the center of each of us. Wherever and whenever such a whorl of patterned sound or space is established in the external world, the power that it contains generates new lines of force whose effects are felt for centuries.

> R.D. Laing
> *The Politics of Experience* (p. 24)

YOUR ESSENTIAL SELF

But you, practical man, have lived all your days amongst the illusions of multiplicity . . . Ambitions and affections, tastes and prejudices, are fighting for your attention. Your poor, worried consciousness flies to and fro amongst them; it has become a restless and a complicated thing. At this very moment your thoughts are buzzing like a swarm of bees. The reduction of this fevered complex to a unity appears to be a task beyond all human power. Yet the situation is not as hopeless for you as it seems. All this is only happening upon the periphery of the mind, where it touches and reacts to the world of appearance. At the centre there is a stillness which even you are not able to break.

There, the rhythm of your duration is one with the rhythm of the Universal Life. There, your essential self exists: the permanent being which persists through and behind the flow and change of your conscious states. You have been snatched to that centre once or twice. Turn your consciousness inward to it deliberately. Retreat to that point whence all the various lines of your activities flow, and to which at last they must return. Since this alone of all that you call your "selfhood" is possessed of eternal reality, it is surely a counsel of prudence to acquaint yourself with its peculiarities and its powers. "Take your seat within the heart of the thousand-petaled lotus," cries the Eastern visionary. "Hold thou to thy Centre," says his Christian brother, "and all things shall be thine." This is a practical recipe, not a pious exhortation. The thing may sound absurd to you, but you can do it if you will: standing back, as it were, from the vague and purposeless reactions in which most men fritter their vital energies.

Evelyn Underhill
Practical Mysticism (pp. 37-39)

REBIRTHING INTO WHOLENESS

There is only one miracle in the world, that of being reborn from division into wholeness. And whether the technique by which this is made possible is called psychological or religious or neither, its object is to remove the obstacles which prevent this perennial miracle from occurring, moment by moment, on every level of our being.

Hugh L'Anson Fausset
Fruits of Silence (p. 107)

PRACTICING SILENCE

The first time Rabbi Mendel, the son of the zaddik of Vorki, met Rabbi Eleazar, the grandson of the maggid of Koznitz, the two retired to a room. They seated themselves opposite each other and sat in silence for a whole hour. Then they admitted the others. "Now we are ready," said Rabbi Mendel.

- - - - - -

When Mendel was in Kotzk, the rabbi of that town asked him: "Where did you learn the art of silence?" He was on the verge of answering the question, but he then changed his mind, and practiced his art.

Martin Buber
Tales of the Hasidim: The Later Masters (p. 301)

LOOKING FOR SOMETHING DEEPER

In the face of wide publicity and much misuse of psychedelic drugs for the expansion of consciousness and the realization of a mystical experience, the Christian pastor and theologian today is given cause for thought and prompted to ask, "What is it today that narrows the consciousness of people to such a great degree that they would go to such desperate means to 'deepen and widen' their spiritual lives?" Only passing attention is given to this in the literature on these drugs. Primary attention is needed. Most of the people who received these experiences have come from a "non-mystical background" of conventional church life and have moved through the nature and nurture approaches to Christian life and education with little or no widening of their consciousness, traumatic or dramatic self-encounter, or discovery of the inner world. Middle class conformity to religion as the expected thing to do has inoculated them against "being fanatical about religion" or "reporting intimations of immortality" which they experience.

Furthermore, the classical means of inducing deeper religious experience are not a part of the Western Protestant tradition. For example, fasting is largely a secular activity motivated by the need to wear last year's clothes comfortably and by vanity to retain one's youth: we diet; we do not fast and meditate on a rooftop someplace in communion with the Holy Spirit. Neither do we have dreams and visions of "the heaven opened and something descending, like a great sheet, let down by four corners upon the earth."

This was the experience the Apostle Peter had when he saw all kinds of animals and reptiles and birds of the air, and was invited to kill and eat. When he refused he was told that God had cleansed this, and what God had cleansed he must not make common. Nor do we have time to stop when we have such an experience and ponder it as did Simon Peter. Therefore, the Spirit does not speak to us and give us guidance as it did the Apostle Peter.

> Wayne E. Oates
> *The Holy Spirit in Five Worlds*
> (pp. 20-21)

FINDING SILENCE

Where shall the word be found, where will the word Resound? Not here, there is not enough silence
> T.S. Eliot
> "Ash Wednesday"

MOVING INTO SILENCE

Another item in the price to be paid is that of sustained effort; the Presence of God, as Thomas à Kempis well knew, cannot be realized without practice. The cult of the Living Silence entails hard work, perseverance, and self-discipline. It is not easy for us to withdraw from the world of sense and thought into the deep quiet where alone we can accept the Divine Gift. We have to train ourselves in the practice and endure courageously long periods of apparent barrenness and failure. Above all we must avoid measuring the success of our communion by the emotional "kick" we get out of it. Communion with God is not primarily a matter of emotion any more than of sense; it is a matter of fact. Sometimes, indeed often, His touch upon our spirit is so light that only afterwards do we realize that He has been with us. Even if we do not realize it at all it does not matter; we are not dependent upon feelings. We belong to God and He belongs to us; we give ourselves to Him and He gives Himself to us, there are no "ifs" or "buts" about it.

Communion with God in the Living Silence is not a substitute for "active" prayer and meditation, rather it is their crown. All three, and a deal of hard, clear thinking in addition, are necessary if the Christian is to achieve a balanced spiritual life. But as, through long discipline, the way into the Silence becomes easier and more habitual the Christian finds that these other activities are constantly leading him up to the inner gateway through which he may plunge, in an instant, into the arms of God. It becomes the natural thing as opportunity occurs during the day to retreat for a few moments into the unseen world of eternity where moments are neither few nor many. Outward noise soon ceases to be a hindrance to the Living Silence; it is not the clatter of a tram-car or the swaying of a crowded bus that interferes so much as the clatter of our thoughts and the swaying of our insatiable desires. But at the beginning the way must be sought with patience and ample time set aside for its practice.

Geoffrey Hoyland
The Use of Silence (pp. 16-18)

WILLING TO PRAY

But there is no compulsion to pray: we can freely decide to pray or to neglect prayer. When we say that prayer is necessary, we mean necessary for the highest part of man's nature; and just as the highest part of man — his soul — is often ignored, so too is prayer. For prayer is not easy. It is not the speaking of many words, or the hypnotic spell of the recited formula; it is the raising of the heart and mind to God in constantly renewed acts of love. We must go forward to grapple with prayer, as Jacob wrestled with the angel. We must lift high our lamp of Faith that it may show us what prayer is, and what are its power and dignity. Into the darkness we must whisper our prayer: *Lord, teach us how to pray.*

The idea is sometimes entertained that we know what prayer is, that we know how to pray, and that therefore we have simply to put our knowledge into practice. However, like so many other ideas which we regard as ordinary currency of knowledge — ideas about the nature of kindness, generosity, charity, silence, understanding, and so forth — our ideas of what prayer is and how we should pray are far from clear. We must question those ideas and thereby come to realize that, so far from the idea of prayer being something which leaps to us spontaneously from the front line of obvious ideas, it is a concept which it will take us our whole life to fathom, and a practice which our whole life will be too short to perfect.

Karl Rahner
On Prayer (pp. 7-8)

COMING HOME

All things have a home, the bird has a nest, the fox has a hole, the bee has a hive. A soul without prayer is a soul without a home. Weary, sobbing, the soul after roving, roaming through a world pestered with aimlessness, falsehoods, absurdities, seeks a moment in which to gather up its scattered trivialized life, in which to divest itself of enforced pretensions and camouflage, in which to simplify complexities, in which to call for help without being a coward — such a home is prayer. Continuity, permanence, intimacy, authenticity, earnestness are its attributes. For the soul, home is where prayer is.

Everybody must build his own home; everybody must guard the independence and the privacy of his prayers. It is the source of security for the integrity of conscience, for whatever inkling we attain of eternity.

At home I have a father who judges and cares, who has regard for me, and when I fail and go astray, misses me. I will never give up my home.

What is a soul without prayer? A soul runaway or a soul evicted from its own home.

How marvellous is my home. I enter as a suppliant and emerge as a witness; I enter as a stranger and emerge as next of kin. I may enter spiritually shapeless, inwardly disfigured, and emerge wholly changed. It is in moments of prayer that my image is forged, that my striving is fashioned.

To understand the world you must love your home. It is difficult to perceive luminosity anywhere, if there is not light in my own home. It is in the light of prayer's radiance that I find my way even in the dark. It is prayer that illumines my way.

Abraham J. Heschel
"Hope Through Renewal of the Self"

KNOWING HOW TO PRAY

A hasid told the rabbi of Kotzk about his poverty and troubles. "Don't worry," advised the rabbi. "Pray to God with all your heart, and the merciful Lord will have mercy upon you." "But I don't know how to pray," said the other. Pity surged up in the Rabbi of Kotzk as he looked at him. "Then," he said, "you have indeed a great deal to worry about."

Martin Buber
Tales of the Hasidim: The Later Masters (p. 280)

UNIFYING YOUR SOUL

The man with the divided, complicated, contradictory soul is not helpless: the core of his soul, the divine force in its depths, is capable of acting upon it, changing it, binding the conflicting forces together, amalgamating the diverging elements — is capable of unifying it. This unification must be accomplished before a man undertakes some unusual work. Only with a united soul will he be able so to do it that it becomes not patchwork but work all of a piece.

Martin Buber
The Way of Man (p. 23)

EXERCISE 4:

The Practice of Meditation

1. Continue the exercise of silence.
2. Add to your period of silent recollection a minimum of ten minutes of meditation upon Scripture. Choose a passage of not more than a few verses, or one event in the life of Christ, or one parable, or even a single word. You may find it rewarding to meditate on the same passage for a week. Volumes have been written on the Lord's Prayer — the fruits of the meditations of others — but of much more value to you will be the fruit of your own meditation, though it might comprise but a few short lines. The Word of God becomes in this way a living Word addressed to you — its meaning internalized in your own life.

Having asked for the gift of the Holy Spirit, and before settling into your silent recollection, select your passage for meditation. Do not become discouraged if, in the early weeks, the time seems to have no meaning for you. You are practicing a difficult art for which few of us have had training. If we remind ourselves that meditation on Scripture is the primary way to deepen our relationship with God and to learn from God what we are to do, we find encouragement to persevere. Meditation is not having great thoughts, but loving the words you hear and letting them shape you.

In Old Testament days children leaving for school were given a little scroll of Scripture to tie around their wrists to refer to throughout the day. From your morning meditation choose a Scripture to bind to yourself for the day.

PRACTICING MEDITATION

The Word of Scripture should never stop sounding in your ears and working in you all day long, just like the words of someone you love. And just as you do not analyze the words of someone you love, but accept them as they are said to you, accept the Word of Scripture and ponder it in your heart, as Mary did. That is all. That is meditation. Do not look for new thoughts and connections in the text, as you would if you were preaching! Do not ask "How shall I pass this on?" but, "What does it say to me?" Then ponder this Word long in your heart until it has gone right into you and taken possession of you.

- - - - - -

We begin meditation with a prayer for the Holy Spirit. Then we ask for composure of mind for ourselves and for all those whom we know to be meditating as well. Then we turn to the text. At the end of the meditation we will be in a position to say a prayer of thanksgiving with a full heart.

What about the text, and how long should it be? It has proved useful to meditate for a whole week on a text of approximately 10 to 15 verses. It is not good to meditate on a different text each day, as our receptiveness is not always the same and the texts are usually far too long. Whatever happens, do not take the text on which you are to preach next Sunday. That belongs to sermon preparation. It is a great help for a brotherhood to know that it is gathered round the same text all week long.

The time for meditation is in the morning, before work begins. Half an hour is the minimum time demanded by a proper meditation. Obvious prerequisites are complete external quietness and the intention of allowing oneself to be distracted by nothing, however important.

One activity of Christian brotherhood, unfortunately practiced very rarely, but quite possible, is occasional meditation in twos or more. There is a narrow path here between false pious loquacity and speculative theological discussion. Anyone who takes on the daily practice of meditation at all seriously will soon find himself in considerable difficulty. Meditation and prayer must be practiced long and seriously. The first thing to remember is not to get impatient with yourself. Do not cramp yourself in despair at the wandering of your thoughts. Just sit down each day and wait patiently. If your thoughts keep running away, do not attempt to restrict them. It is no bother to let them run on to their destination; then, however, take up the place or the person to whom they have strayed into your prayers. In this way you will find yourself back at the text, and the minutes of such digressions will not be wasted and will not trouble you.

There are a great many helps which each will seek for his own special difficulties: Read the same saying again and again, write down your thoughts, from time to time learn the verse off by heart (in fact one will be able to have any text that has really been meditated upon off by heart anyway). We will also soon learn the danger of escaping from meditation to biblical scholarship or something else. Behind all the needs and difficulties there really lies our great need of prayer; many of us have remained all too long without any help and instruction.

In the face of this, there is nothing for it but to begin again, faithfully and patiently, the very first practices of prayer and meditation. We will be helped on further by the fact that others are also meditating, that all the time the holy church everywhere, in heaven and on earth, is praying together. This is a comfort in the weakness of prayer. If at any time we really do not know what we are to pray, and are in utter despair about it, we still know that the Holy Spirit is taking our part with sighs that cannot be expressed.

We may never give up this daily concern with Scripture, and must begin it straightaway, if we have not already done so. For it is there that we have eternal life.

Dietrich Bonhoeffer
The Way to Freedom (pp. 59-61)

WAITING ON GOD

It is important that we get still to wait on God. And it is best that we get alone, preferably with our Bible outspread before us. Then if we will we may draw near to God and begin to hear Him speak to us in our hearts. I think for the average person the progression will be something like this: First a sound as of a Presence walking in the garden. Then a voice, more intelligible, but still far from clear. Then the happy moment when the Spirit begins to illuminate the Scriptures, and that which had been only a sound, or at best a voice, now becomes an intelligible word, warm and intimate and clear as the word of a dear friend. Then will come life and light, and best of all, ability to see and rest in and embrace Jesus Christ as Saviour and Lord and All.

The Bible will never be a living Book to us until we are convinced that God is articulate in His universe. To jump from a dead, impersonal world to a dogmatic Bible is too much for most people. They may admit that they *should* accept the Bible as the Word of God, and they may try to think of it as such, but they find it impossible to believe that the words there on the page are actually for them. A man may *say*, "These words are addressed to me," and yet in his heart not feel and know that they are. He is the victim of a divided psychology. He tries to think of God as mute everywhere else and vocal only in a book.

I believe that much of our religious unbelief is due to a wrong conception of and a wrong feeling for the Scriptures of Truth. A silent God suddenly began to speak in a book and when the book was finished lapsed back into silence again forever . . .

I think a new world will arise out of the religious mists when we approach our Bible with the idea that it is not only a book which was once spoken, but a book which is *now speaking.* The prophets habitually said, "Thus *saith* the Lord." They meant their hearers to understand that God's speaking is in the continuous present. We may use the past tense properly to indicate that at a certain time a certain word of God was spoken, but a word of God once spoken continues to be spoken, as a child once born continues to be alive, or a world once created continues to exist. And those are but imperfect illustrations, for children die and worlds burn out, but the Word of our God endureth for-ever.

A. W. Tozer
The Pursuit of God (pp. 80-82)

A METHOD OF MEDITATION

The best over-all preparation for successful meditation is a per-sonal conviction of its importance and a staunch determination to persevere in its practice. If one has acquired this attitude of mind, he has made a splendid preparation for his meditation.

St. Teresa gives us this important admonition:

> It is essential, I maintain, to begin the practice of prayer with a firm resolution to persevere in it.
>
> — St. Teresa, *Way of Perfection,* xxi.

If one be not convinced of the necessity of meditation in his own life, nor resolved never to omit its daily exercise, he will soon give it up on one pretext or another. Therefore, one should not adopt the practice of meditation with the intention of "giving it a try"; but rather, one must undertake the exercise with a firm belief that it is of the utmost importance that he begin and per-severe in it. Our mental attitude towards any enterprise will determine, to a large extent, our success in it; meditation is no exception.

- - - - - -

The modern, twentieth-century man is completely unaccus-tomed to the rarefied air of the interior life, and will certainly wander and stumble if he does not possess an outline to follow. If one begins prayer with this methodical procedure, he can be sure to make progress. St. Teresa is insistent that we attack this prob-lem with a grim determination. And one of the best evidences of good faith in the matter is to proceed systematically to one's conversation with Christ.

- - - - - -

General purpose: to hold loving conversation with Christ.
  1. *Preparation:*
     Place oneself in the presence of Christ.
  2. *Selection of the material:*
     Read; or study a picture of Christ.
  3. *Consideration:*
     Reflect upon the material. Ask oneself the questions: who, what, why, for what reason?
  4. *Conversation: (Core of Meditation)*
     Converse with Our Lord about the material. Employ the affections of love, adoration, thanksgiving, sorrow, petition.
  5. *Conclusion:*
     Gratitude to Christ for favors received. Examination of faults during meditation, and resolution of further effort in succeeding meditations.

Peter-Thomas Rohrbach, O.C.D.
Conversation with Christ
(pp. 31-32, 26-27)

SELECTING YOUR MEDITATION

I will explain myself further, for these matters concerning prayer are difficult, and, if no director is available, very hard to understand. It is for this reason that, though I should like to write more briefly, and though merely to touch upon these matters concerning prayer would suffice for the keen intellect of him who commanded me to write of them, my own stupidity prevents me from describing and explaining in a few words a matter which it is so important to expound thoroughly. Having gone through so much myself, I am sorry for those who begin with books alone, for it is extraordinary what a difference there is between understanding a thing and knowing it by experience. Returning, then to what I was saying, we begin to meditate upon a scene of the Passion — let us say upon the binding of the Lord to the Column. The mind sets to work to seek out the reasons which are to be found for the great afflictions and distress which His Majesty must have suffered when He was alone there. It also meditates on the many other lessons which, if it is industrious, or well stored with learning, this mystery can teach it. This method should be the beginning, the middle and the end of prayer for all of us: it is a most excellent and safe road until the Lord leads us to other methods, which are supernatural.

I say "for all of us," but there will be many souls who derive greater benefits from other meditations than from that of the Sacred Passion. For, just as there are many mansions in Heaven, so there are many roads to them. Some people derive benefit from imagining themselves in hell; others, whom it distresses to think of hell, from imagining themselves in Heaven. Others meditate upon death. Some, who are tender-hearted, get exhausted if they keep thinking about the Passion, but they derive great comfort and benefit from considering the power and greatness of God in the creatures, and the love that He showed us, which is pictured in all things. This is an admirable procedure, provided one does not fail to meditate often upon the Passion and the life of Christ, which are, and have always been, the source of everything that is good.

Saint Teresa of Avila
Life (p. 79)

MEDITATING ON THE PASSION

The story of Christ's passion should be read with brooding insight. We should seek the stimulus of choice devotional books

on this subject. Then at certain times — perhaps on seven con-
secutive days — we should center our attention upon the last
words that He uttered. What unplumbed depth of meaning we
might discover in each phrase! A symbol of the Cross can constantly recall our thoughts to His passion. We should meditate
long upon the great prophetic chapter, Isaiah 53, which, whatever
its original setting may have been, was appropriated by Jesus as
the spiritual picture of His Life. Its words should get into our
memories and into our hearts. There are hymns which pulse with
the meaning of the Cross. Whatever our rule and practice of
prayer may be, there is a need for a deeper apprehension of the
Cross. Let us set apart some sacred prayer period on every Friday
to center our gaze on Calvary and thus keep it as a Day of the
Cross.

It would be a deepening experience for every one of us to lay
out a course of meditation that would enable us to pray our way
into the great mysteries of Christ's life. Teresa said concerning her
meditations:

> This was my method of prayer; as I could not make
> reflections with my understanding, I contrived to
> picture Christ within me; and I used to find myself the
> better for thinking of those mysteries of His life dur-
> ing which He was most lonely . . . I did many simple
> things of this kind; and in particular I used to find
> myself most at home in the prayer of the Garden,
> whither I went in His company. I wished, if it had
> been possible, to wipe away that painful sweat from
> His face. . . I believe my soul gained very much in this
> way, because I began to practice prayer without
> knowing what it was.
>
> —*Life,* IX. 4: cf. IV. 10.

To picture vividly and appreciate vitally the experiences of the
Upper Room, the Garden, the Trial, and the Cross surely would
draw us nearer to an understanding of His passion.

Lynn James Radcliffe
Making Prayer Real (pp. 213-214)

RESISTING DISTRACTIONS

But, the choice made, it must be held and defended during the time of meditation against all invasions from without, however insidious their encroachments, however "spiritual" their disguise. It must be brooded upon, gazed at, seized again and again, as distractions seem to snatch it from your grasp. A restless boredom, a dreary conviction of your own incapacity, will presently attack you. This, too, must be resisted at swordpoint. The first quarter of an hour thus spent in attemped meditation will be, indeed, a time of warfare; which should at least convince you how unruly, how ill-educated is your attention, how miserably ineffective your will, how far away you are from the captaincy of your own soul.

Evelyn Underhill
Practical Mysticism (pp. 51-52)

CONCENTRATION

This device is as a rule the practice of meditation, in which the state of Recollection usually begins: that is to say, the deliberate consideration of and dwelling upon some one aspect of Reality — an aspect most usually chosen from amongst the religious beliefs of the self. Thus Hindu mystics will brood upon a sacred word, whilst Christian contemplatives set before their minds one of the names or attributes of God, a fragment of Scripture, an incident of the life of Christ; and allow — indeed encourage — this consideration, and the ideas and feelings which flow from it, to occupy the whole mental field. This powerful suggestion, kept before the consciousness by an act of will, overpowers the stream of small suggestions which the outer world pours incessantly upon the mind. The self, concentrated upon this image or idea, dwelling on it more than thinking about it — as one may gaze upon a picture that one loves — falls gradually and insensibly into the condition of reverie; and, protected by this holy day-dream from the more distracting dream of life, sinks into itself, and becomes in the language of asceticism "recollected" or gathered together.

Evelyn Underhill
Mysticism (p. 314)

BEYOND THINKING

The masters of the spiritual life advise that we should, when contemplating, make use of our imagination. For example, we should visualize an incident such as the miracle of the draught of fishes as vividly as we can. We should be present in mind as though we had just stopped on our way and were witnessing the event. This is most useful because it brings the event to life and makes it part of our inner experience. Of course, not everybody is able to do that. Many people completely lack the power of imagination and might not even be able to visualize the scene. Others lack the power to hold it, so that it quickly dissolves. They should not force themselves, but should rely more on thinking without visualization.

Thinking is also important for the person with a vivid imagination. The term "contemplate" means to reflect on and carefully work through a subject. This is what we should do with the chosen text. In this manner should we endeavor to acquaint ourselves with it and to penetrate into its deeper meaning.

However — we have mentioned this before — we should not approach this text as though it were a scientific problem, with our intellect only: our heart must take part in it. Thinking must change into pondering, reflecting, entering and contacting; thinking must go beyond thinking, for the truth which we are trying to apprehend is wisdom which we might define as knowledge of the heart and instructedness of the whole of our being.

Romano Guardini
Prayer in Practice (pp. 102-103)

IMAGINATION

. . . represent to your imagination the whole of the mystery on which you desire to meditate was if it really passed in your presence. For example, if you wish to meditate on our Lord on the Cross, imagine that you are on Mount Calvary, and that you there behold and hear all that was done or said on the day of the Passion. Or, if you prefer it, for it is all one, imagine that in the very place where you are they are crucifying our Lord in the manner described by the holy evangelists. I say the same thing when you meditate on death, as I have noted in the meditation upon it, and so also on hell, or on any like mystery in which visible and sensible objects form a part of the subject. As to other mysteries, such as relate to the greatness of God, the excellency of the virtues, or the end for which we were created, which are invisible things, there is no question of using this kind of imagination. It is true that we may use some similitude or comparison to assist us in the consideration of these subjects, but this is attended with some difficulty. My intention is to instruct you in so plain and easy a manner that your mind may not be burdened too much with making such devices.

By means of the imagination we confine our mind within the mystery on which we meditate, that it may not ramble to and fro, just as we shut up a bird in a cage or tie a hawk by his leash so that he may rest on the hand. Some may perhaps tell you that it is better to use the simple thought of faith and to conceive the subject in a manner entirely mental and spiritual in the representation of the mysteries, or else to imagine that the things take place in your own soul. This method is too subtle for beginners. Therefore, until God raises you higher, Philothea, I advise you to remain in the low valley which I have shown you.

- - - - - -

... Do like the bees, who never quit a flower so long as they can extract any honey from it. If, after a little hesitation and trial, you do not succeed with one consideration according to your wishes, proceed to another. But go calmly and tranquilly in this matter without hurrying yourself.

St. Francis de Sales
Introduction to the Devout Life
(pp. 83-84)

PRAYING A PSALM

Another simple way of meditation is to take a Psalm: try to think out the situation from which the psalmist wrote; you can be as simple and natural about this as possible; you will find how very "modern" are the situations from which these great prayers or hymns sprang. Apply what you find to your own life and its present circumstances. Then turn the Psalm into a prayer, repeating it slowly and thoughtfully.

Whatever method of meditation is chosen there are three special considerations to bear in mind:

(a) Always begin with prayer; remember the Presence of God, and ask for the guidance and teaching of the Holy Spirit.

(b) If your thoughts wander, bring them back gently to God. Do not get discouraged by difficulties.

(c) Always end a meditation with a short prayer and a practical resolution; the latter should be something possible to do on that actual day.

Olive Wyon
The School of Prayer (p. 104)

THE IMPORTANCE OF LISTENING

I did not send the prophets,
    yet they ran;
I did not speak to them,
    yet they prophesied.
But if they had stood in my council,
    then they would have proclaimed
        my words to my people
and they would have turned them
    from their evil way,
and from the evil of their doings.

            Jeremiah 23: 21-23, *RSV*

HUNGER FOR GOD

Many people are prepared to have faith in the sense of scientifically indefensible belief in an untested hypothesis. Few have trust enough to test it. Many people make-believe what they experience. Few are made to believe by their experience. Paul of Tarsus was picked up by the scruff of the neck, thrown to the ground and blinded for three days. This direct experience was self-validating.

We live in a secular world. To adapt to this world the child abdicates its ecstasy. ("L'enfant abdique son extase": Mallarmé.) Having lost our experience of the spirit, we are expected to have faith. But this faith comes to be a belief in a reality which is not evident. There is a prophecy in Amos that a time will come when there will be a famine in the land, "not a famine for bread, nor a thirst for water, but of *hearing* the words of the Lord." That time has now come to pass. It is the present age.

        R. D. Laing
        The Politics of Experience
        (pp. 100-101)

GROWING WITH MEDITATION

Happy is the man
    who does not take the wicked for his guide
    nor walk the road that sinners tread
    nor take his seat among the scornful;
    the law of the the Lord is his delight,
the law his meditation night and day.
        He is like a tree
    planted beside a watercourse,
    which yields its fruit in season
        and its leaf never withers:
    in all that he does he prospers.

Psalm 1:1-3, NEB

EXERCISE 5:
Contemplative Prayer and the Created Order

1. Practice your exercise of silent recollection.
2. Meditate on Scripture for not less than ten minutes each day. If you are tempted to shorten the time, lengthen it, even if only by one minute. Remember that in the beginning these exercises are toil.
3. Choose something in the created order and, for five minutes each day, practice the outpouring of yourself toward it. It does not matter what you choose — a cup of water, a slice of bread, a leaf, a tree, a building, a piece of machinery. Then, using your will, energy and powers of concentration defend the object chosen against all other claims for your attention. Employ your senses — sight, hearing, touch, and smell.

This may seem like an odd assignment, but to become a contemplative person one must know how to look. Although in this sense, all of us have had the contemplative experience at some time in our lives, for the person whose powers of attention have been sharpened in a given area the experience is probably better known. Artists seeing a segment of their world with heightened perception are in those moments contemplative persons. Their paintings are not only what they have seen, but what they have experienced, and thus, when we really look at their works, our own experience is widened. The fact is, however, that we seldom look intently. Even visitors to art galleries seem to have nothing in themselves which equips them to see. They just walk through. "They don't see what is in front of them — if it doesn't grab them, they go away," says Mrs. Ruth Bowman, a lecturer at the Museum of Modern Art in New York. "People who come to museums don't really enjoy anything," says John Walker, former director of the National Art Gallery in Washington. "They don't look at works of art long enough." Children who fasten their gazes in awe upon an insect and scientists who look through microscopes with their whole beings are what we mean by contemplatives. We find a few in every area of activity.

CONTEMPLATING NATURE

To elude nature, to refuse her friendship, and attempt to leap the river of life in the hope of finding God on the other side, is the common error of a perverted mysticality. It is as fatal in result as the opposite error of deliberately arrested development, which, being attuned to the wonderful rhythms of natural life, is content with this increase of sensibility; and, becoming a "nature-mystic," asks no more.

So you are to begin with that first form of contemplation which the old mystics sometimes called the "discovery of God in His creatures."

- - - - - -

Begin therefore at once. Gather yourself up, as the exercises of recollection have taught you to do. Then — with attention no longer frittered amongst the petty accidents and interests of your personal life, but poised, tense, ready for the work you shall demand of it — stretch out by a distinct act of loving will towards one of the myriad manifestations of life that surround you: and which, in an ordinary way, you hardly notice unless you happen to need them. Pour yourself out towards it, do not draw its image towards you. Deliberate — more, impassioned — attentiveness, an attentiveness which soon transcends all consciousness of yourself, as separate from and attending to the thing seen; this is the condition of success. As to the object of contemplation, it matters little. From Alp to insect, anything will do, provided that your attitude be right: for all things in this world towards which you are stretching out are linked together, and one truly apprehended will be the gateway to the rest.

- - - - - -

Such a simple exercise, if entered upon with singleness of heart, will soon repay you. By this quiet yet tense act of communion, this loving gaze, you will presently discover a relationship — far more intimate than anything you imagined — between yourself and the surrounding "objects of sense"; and in those objects of sense a profound significance, a personal quality, and actual

- - - - - -

power of response, which you might in cooler moments think absurd.   - - - - -

Further, you will observe that this act, and the attitude which is proper to it, differs in a very important way even from that special attentiveness which characterized the stage of meditation, and which seems at first sight to resemble it in many respects. Then, it was an idea or image from amongst the common stock — one of those conceptual labels with which the human pastebrush has decorated the surface of the universe — which you were encouraged to hold before your mind. Now, turning away from the label, you shall surrender yourself to the direct message poured out towards you by the *thing*. Then, you considered: now, you are to absorb. This experience will be, in the very highest sense, the experience of sensation without thought . . .

Evelyn Underhill
Practical Mysticism
(pp. 90-91,93-94,95,98-99)

TRUE SEEING TRANSFORMS

A real artist is a creator and not a copyist. He has visited God's workshop and has learned the secrets of creation — creating something out of nothing.

With such a painter every stroke of his brush is the work of creation, and it cannot be retraced because it never permits a repetition. God cannot cancel his fiat; it is final, irrevocable, it is an ultimatum. The painter cannot reproduce his own work. When even a single stroke of his brush is absolute, how can the whole structure or composition be reproduced, since this is the synthesis of all his strokes, every one of which has been directed towards the whole?

In the same way every minute of human life as long as it is an expression of its inner self is original, divine, creative, and cannot be retrieved. Each individual life thus is a great work of art. Whether or not one makes it a fine inimitable masterpiece depends upon one's consciousness of the working of *śūnyatā* within oneself.

How does the painter get into the spirit of the plant, for instance, if he wants to paint a hibiscus as Mokkei (Muchi) of the thirteenth century did in his famous picture, which is now preserved as a national treasure at Daitokuji temple in Kyoto? The secret is to become the plant itself. But how can a human being turn himself into a plant? Inasmuch as he aspires to paint a plant or an animal, there must be in him something which corresponds to it in one way or another. If so, he ought to be able to become the object he desires to paint.

The discipline consists in studying the plant inwardly with his mind thoroughly purified of its subjective, self-centered contents. This means to keep the mind in unison with the "Emptiness" or Suchness, whereby one who stands against the object ceases to be the one outside that object but transforms himself into the object itself. This identification enables the painter to feel the pulsation of one and the same life animating both him and the object. This is what is meant when it is said that the subject is lost in the object, and that when the painter begins his work it is not he but the object itself that is working and it is then that his brush, as well as his arm and his fingers, become obedient servants to the spirit of the objects. The object makes its own picture. The spirit sees itself as reflected in itself. This is also a case of self-identity.

It is said that Henri Matisse looked at an object which he intended to paint for weeks, even for months, until its spirit began to move him, to urge him, even to threaten him, to give it an expression.

D. T. Suzuki
Mysticism: Christian and Buddhist (pp. 34-35)

FACE TO FACE WITH CREATION

I have had the experience of living in a false world. One day I was deeply depressed by the severe criticisms a colleague had received — a person who was living his life in an honest and truthful sense, attempting to express his unique interests in his work. I felt especially saddened when I realized how he had suffered, when all he wanted to do was maintain a personal and creative identity, a genuine existence and relatedness. I felt especially sensitive to pretense and surface behavior, as though nothing were real. A numbness settled in, right at the center of my thought and feeling. That night even the children were unable to shake my grief and sadness. In their own spontaneous, unknowing ways, they tugged and pulled at me to draw me into life but for me there remained only suffering in the world.

After the children had gone to bed, I decided to go for a walk. The night was dark, filled with black clouds. Large white flakes of snow fell on and around me. The night was silent and serene. Suddenly, without understanding in any way, I experienced a transcendental beauty in the white darkness. It was difficult to walk on the glazed surface but as I walked I felt drawn to the black, inky streaks embedded in the ice. Dark, wavy lines, partly covered by snow, spread out in grotesque forms. I knelt down, touching the black, irregular patterns. Immediately I felt a chill but at the same time the ice began melting as my fingers touched it.

My inward heaviness lifted, and I was restored to a new capacity for exertion and endurance. I realized how, out of broken roots and fibers, in a genuine encounter with natural resources, it is possible to discover a new level of individual identity and to develop new strength and conviction. I realized how the self can be shattered in surface and false meetings when surrounded by intensive pressures to conform, and how in communion with nature the self can reach a new dimension of optimism and a new recognition of the creative way of life. Possibilities for unique and unusual meetings exist everywhere. We need only reach out in natural covering to come face to face with creation.

Clark Moustakas
Creativity and Conformity
(pp. 41-42)

MIRACLES

Monsieur Tabourel's teaching was far from exciting. It was during one of his lessons that a privet hawk-moth chose the time for coming out of its chrysalis. I had reared the caterpillar and was keeping the chrysalis carefully in the small narrow uncovered box, in which it lay looking like a mummy in its sarcophagus. I used to examine it every day, but never perceived the smallest change, and I should perhaps have despaired if it had not been for the little convulsive movements this semblance of a creature made when I tickled its abdomen with the nib of my pen. It was really alive then! Now on that day, as Monsieur Tabourel was correcting my sums, my eyes fell on the box. O Proteus! What did I see? Wings! Great green and pink wings beginning to stir and quiver!

Overwhelmed with admiration, with joy, dancing with enthusiasm, I could not help seizing, for want of a better divinity, old Tabourel's fat paw.

"Oh, Monsieur Tabourel! Look! Oh, if had only known . . ."

I stopped short just in time, for what I had been meaning to say was: "If I had only known that while you were explaining those deadly sums, one of the mysteries of life, so great a one, so long expected, was going on at my very elbow! . . ." A resurrection like Lazarus's! A metamorphosis, a miracle I had never yet beheld . . .

Monsieur Tabourel was a man of education; calmly, but with a shade of astonishment or blame or something disapproving in his voice:

"What!" said he; "didn't you know that a chrysalis is the envelope of a butterfly? Every butterfly you see has come out of a chrysalis. It's perfectly natural."

At that I dropped Monsieur Tabourel's hand. Yes indeed, I knew my *natural* history as well, perhaps better than he . . . But because it was natural, could he not see that it was marvellous? Poor creature! From that day, I took a dislike to him and a loathing to his lessons.

André Gide
If It Die (p. 83)

SILENT VOICES

To the silent awareness, the skinny cat is all cat, the very essence of cat. Its sneaky feline motions are all of a piece, speaking directly to the consciousness in soundless tones of all that cat means, of cat in past, present, future. The eternal cat.

And even buildings . . .

They have less to say than cats but they communicate. They almost turn themselves inside out in their eagerness to share their secrets. They tell of the men that made them, the beings that dwell in them; indeed, they portray a whole history of architecture but again without words, without discourse, all in an instant, for time itself, in this silent world, attains a new dimension — the eternal Now — in which millennia can be experienced as instants.

Robert S. de Ropp
The Master Game (p. 72)

VOYAGE OF DISCOVERY

A pair of wings, a different mode of breathing, which would enable us to traverse infinite space, would in no way help us, for if we visited Mars or Venus keeping the same senses, they would clothe in the same aspect as the things of the earth everything that we should be capable of seeing. The only true voyage of discovery, the only fountain of Eternal Youth, would be not to visit strange lands but to possess other eyes, to behold the universe through the eyes of another, of a hundred others, to behold the hundred universes that each of them beholds, that each of them is.

Marcel Proust
Remembrance of Things Past
(p. 559)

SEEING

But each for the joy of the working
And each, in his separate star,
Shall draw the Thing as he sees It
For the God of Things as They are!

Rudyard Kipling
"When Earth's Last Picture Is Painted"

CATCHING THE REFLECTION

Odysseus' great dog Argos, abused and cast out on a dung heap, wagged his tail and was the first to recognize his old master after nineteen years of absence. In a like way Darwin's favorite dog recognized him after his five-year absence on the *Beagle*.

It is not necessary to cavil over the great age of Odysseus' dog. The surprising thing about the story's descent through the millennia is that it comes from a fierce and violent era, yet it bespeaks some recognized bond between man and beast. The tie runs beyond the cities into some remote glade in a far forest where man willingly accepted the help of his animal kin. Though men in the mass forget the origins of their need, they still bring wolfhounds into city apartments, where dog and man both sit brooding in wistful discomfort.

- - - - - -

The magic that gleams an instant between Argos and Odysseus is both the recognition of diversity and the need for affection across the illusions of form. It is nature's cry to homeless, far-wandering, insatiable man: "Do not forget your brethren, nor the green wood from which you sprang. To do so is to invite disaster."

- - - - - -

. . . Plotinus wrote of the soul's journey, "It shall come, not to another, but to itself." It is possible to add that for the soul to come to its true self it needs the help and recognition of the dog Argos. It craves that empathy clinging between man and beast, that nagging shadow of remembrance which, try as we may to deny it, asserts our unity with life and does more. Paradoxically, it establishes, in the end, our own humanity. One does not meet oneself until one catches the reflection from an eye other than human.

Loren Eiseley
The Unexpected Universe
(pp. 23,24)

PRESSING TOWARD THE TRUE

Yet toward what do most of our citizens work? What beacons do they follow? One has only to ask the question "What is provided for us?" to realize that our advanced nations are made up of pleasure-seekers. Manufactures and services are designed for our pleasure, and advertising is designed to remind us continually of the pleasures we are (rightly) thought to desire. Our habitual response to this constant pressure is to work with extreme diligence to achieve the financial success required to buy these "goods."

So far there seems to be no problem: I have described a commercial system which thoroughly "satisfies" the customer. In point of fact, however, the customer is *not* satisfied. After radio he must have television, inevitably to be followed by color. After Michigan wine, he must have Californian, and then French; after Chevrolet and Dodge, then Cadillac. Still, these things do not well satisfy, for the simple reason that they are not crucial needs. Since many things are too easily achieved, there is no great relaxation of tension when they are obtained. The pleasure gained is only shallow and brief, and the flood of advertising soon convinces us of new needs to replace the old.

Due to the awareness of striving to be happy, to have a pleasure which we have not achieved, we quickly notice its early disappearance. For the first few times the pain is simple, but later on it becomes far deeper and more complex: at first frustrated, then resentful, to become, perhaps, even anxious or neurotic. Why, for instance, do the richest countries in the world have the highest rates of mental disease? The answer is clear: under the scream of advertising there is a steady whine of frustration: "I'm not happy; *make me happy!*" Yet even when this can be done, happiness is not success. Happiness is only a sign of success, and without a preceding obstacle or need which has been overcome in struggle, it is hollow indeed.

And yet the avoidance of discomfort seems so natural and beneficial to us that it would sound foolish indeed to advise otherwise. What direction should we take, then? What goal shall we seek?

Richard O. Whipple
"The View from Zorna"

SPENDING YOURSELF

The world is too much with us; late and soon,
Getting and spending, we lay waste our powers:
Little we see in Nature that is ours.

William Wordsworth
"The World is Too Much With Us"

ONENESS

For a long time I stood close to the brink, clinging to a stunted Fraser fir. Hardly a dozen feet high, it had been twisted and distorted by the wind. All its branches streamed in one direction, back from the edge of the escarpment. Like some green Winged Victory it clung there, bearing the brunt of the storm. I could feel the tremors running down its toughened wood as the great gusts struck. This was an old story for it. Its world was a harsher, windier world than that of the lowland trees. It was blighted, but still alive; it had endured, altered but unbroken by adversity. I have often thought of that steadfast tree. A fragment of one of its twigs lies before me as I write. On that day with fog streaming past us, with the wind howling over us, feeling the tremors run through the fibers of its trunk and down my arm, facing the gale as it had faced so many gales, I felt an overpowering oneness with this storm-racked tree. And never have I felt myself in better or more noble company.

Edwin Way Teale
North with the Spring (p. 205)

DISCOVERY IN SOLITUDE

But, you see, you are not educated to be alone. Do you ever go out for a walk by yourself? It is very important to go out alone, to sit under a tree — not with a book, not with a companion, but by yourself — and observe the falling of a leaf, hear the lapping of the water, the fisherman's song, watch the flight of the bird, and of your own thoughts as they chase each other across the space of your mind. If you are able to be alone and watch these things, then you will discover extraordinary riches which no government can tax, no human agency can corrupt, and which can never be destroyed.

J. Krishnamurti
Think on These Things (p. 89)

CREATION AND RE-CREATION

There is an intimate link between creativity and contemplation, although the current tendency is to oppose them. Contemplation must not be understood as a state of sheer passivity or receptiveness: it comprises a distinctly active and creative element. Thus the aesthetic contemplation of natural beauty is more than a state: it is an act, a breaking through to another world.

Beauty is indeed that other world revealing itself in our own. And in contemplating beauty man goes out to meet its call. A poet who is possessed by his vision of beauty is not engaged in passive observation but in an activity whereby he creates for himself and re-creates in his imagination the image of beauty. Contemplation does, admittedly, preclude the experience of struggle, conflict and opposition. But it supplies that background against which struggle, conflict and opposition acquire significance. Man ought to be able from time to time to fall back on contemplation in order to obtain relief from the activism of existence which, as we know too well today, can tear him to pieces.

Nicolas Berdyaev
Dream and Reality (p. 215-216)

LEARNING THE SONG

After the maggid's death, his disciples came together and talked about the things he had done. When it was Rabbi Schneur Zalman's turn, he asked them: "Do you know why our master went to the pond every day at dawn and stayed there for a little while before coming home again?" They did not know why. Rabbi Zalman continued: "He was learning the song with which the frogs praise God. It takes a very long time to learn that song."

Martin Buber
Tales of the Hasidim: The Early Masters (p. lll)

THE CRY OF THE HILLS

Before you
mountains and hills shall break into cries of joy,
and all the trees of the wild
shall clap their hands . . .

Isaiah 55:12, *NEB*

THE ULTIMATE DREAMER

I saw, had many times seen, both mentally and in the seams of exposed strata, the long backward stretch of time whose recovery is one of the great feats of modern science. I saw the drifting cells of the early seas from which all life, including our own, has arisen. The salt of those ancient seas is in our blood, its lime is in our bones. Every time we walk along a beach some ancient urge disturbs us so that we find ourselves shedding shoes and garments, or scavenging among seaweed and whitened timbers like the homesick refugees of a long war.

- - - - - -

We are too content with our sensory extensions, with the fulfillment of that ice age mind that began its journey amidst the cold of vast tundras and that pauses only briefly before its leap into space. It is no longer enough to see as a man sees — even to the ends of the universe. It is not enough to hold nuclear energy in one's hand like a spear, as a man would hold it, or to see the lightning, or times past, or time to come, as a man would see it. If we continue to do this, the great brain — the human brain — will be only a new version of the old trap, and nature is full of traps for the beast that cannot learn.

It is not sufficient any longer to listen at the end of a wire to the rustlings of galaxies; it is not enough even to examine the great coil of DNA in which is coded the very alphabet of life. These are our extended perceptions. But beyond lies the great darkness of the ultimate Dreamer, who dreamed the light and the galaxies. Before act was, or substance existed, imagination grew in the dark. Man partakes of that ultimate wonder and creativeness. As we turn from the galaxies to the swarming cells of our own being, which toil for something, some entity beyond their grasp, let us remember man, the self-fabricator who came across an ice age to look into the mirrors and the magic of science. Surely he did not come to see himself or his wild visage only. He came because he is at heart a listener and a searcher for some transcendent realm beyond himself. This he has worshipped by many names, even in the dismal caves of his beginning. Man, the self-fabricator, is so by reason of gifts he had no part in devising — and so he searches as the single living cell in the beginning must have sought the ghostly creature it was to serve.

Loren Eiseley
The Unexpected Universe
(pp. 51, 54-55)

EXERCISE 6:

Contemplative Prayer
and the Indwelling God

1. Continue the exercise of silence.
2. Meditate on Scripture for ten minutes or more.
3. Practice contemplation for a minimum of ten minutes: take the attention which you have directed toward a truer apprehension of something in the created order, and turn it toward the Silence deep within you. Do not use words, or pictures, or your senses, but only your "naked intent unto God."

The writings which follow will give you incentive and help. You will have to overcome strong resistances in your effort to put everything else out of your mind and concentrate your attention on God, and God *only*. One of the intruding questions that will cross your mind is, "Have I put in the required time?" — so eager will you be to finish with the exercise. That question is an indication that you have not reached your silent Self, because when you are there you will be taken hold of and find it hard to leave. In time you will not have to struggle to reach that place where you look at God and God looks at you.

Remember that the following selections are like small sectors of large maps. If you have other readings that are more helpful to you, by all means use them. If you have not already done so, I would recommend that at some time you read the whole of *The Cloud of Unknowing* in a modern translation, provided, of course, that you heed the author's plea in his prologue. Another comprehensive and important volume is Evelyn Underhill's large work entitled *Mysticism*. But do not read as a substitute for practicing the exercise. Read when you are in need of something that will pull your heart into prayer.

CONDITION OF SIMPLICITY

Now, in the second stage, the disciplined and recollected attention seems to take an opposite course. It is directed towards a plane of existence with which your bodily senses have no attachments: which is not merely misrepresented by your ordinary concepts, but cannot be represented by them at all. It must therefore sink inwards towards its own centre, "away from all that can be thought or felt," as the mystics say, "away from every image, every notion, every thing," towards that strange condition of obscurity which St. John of the Cross calls the "Night of Sense." Do this steadily, checking each vagrant instinct, each insistent thought, however "spiritual" it may seem; pressing ever more deeply inwards toward that ground, that simple and undifferentiated Being from which your diverse faculties emerge. Presently you will find yourself, emptied and freed, in a place stripped bare of all the machinery of thought; and achieve the condition of simplicity which those same specialists call nakedness of spirit or "Wayless Love," and which they declare to be above all human images and ideas — a state of consciousness in which "all the workings of the reason fail." Then you will observe that you have entered into an intense and vivid silence: a silence which exists in itself, through and in spite of the ceaseless noises of your normal world.

Evelyn Underhill
Practical Mysticism (pp. 119-120)

STILLNESS

"Be still, and know that I am God . . ."
Psalm 46:10, *RSV*

GOD IN YOU

. . . Jung writes: . . .

"When the libido is withdrawn from the outer object and sinks into the unconscious, the 'soul is born in God.' " Here is an interesting combination of psychological and religious language. Has analytical psychology something to say to us regarding such an elemental aspect of religion as this? The soul is our meeting place with God. And the soul is born in God when we become aware that our psyche is inseparable from God whose image is its center. So when we withdraw from the world — introvert, in other words — the libido that once flowed from us, outward, to the world and things now flows inward and activates the soul. God responds to this inner activation by drawing near and ultimately being born in us, that is, his presence is consciously recognized and acknowledged.

Here in a capsule, is the psychology of religious experience. It no longer need be seen as a haphazard matter; it follows quite definite laws of our psychic nature. Here then is the meaning of religious retreats, of silence, of monastic withdrawal. They are the means by which, through a turning away from externals, the interior life is activated. This is the treasure hid in a field, the pearl of great price . . . These are symbolic expressions for something that is hidden deep within us. They are not make-believe; they belong to the equipment of our souls, and require only an earnest, inward quest on our part for us to find them.

But to do so requires the recognition that our soul, our "inwardness" is such that God can indwell, and that even the squalor of the manger of our instincts and passions he can organize and use for his glory. In his holiness he does not abhor the lowliness of our instinctual life. It is because we tend to think of God as so high above us that he is altogether removed from these aspects of our living — too holy to look upon them other than as sin — that we have lost the sense of his nearness and intimacy. This is why both Jung and Eckhart stress the importance of having God in us, as contrasted to our simply being in God. "That God is in the soul is an higher estate than that the soul is in God," writes Eckhart.

"When the soul is in God, it is not blessed therein, but blessed indeed is the soul which God inhabits. Of this be ye certain: *"God is Himself blessed in the soul."* The difference is the difference between the Old Testament and the New. The Old Testament men and women were, for the most part, aware of God, overawed by his power and majesty, but there was no blessing in it compared with the blessing that comes when God is incarnate, i.e., born in man — first, in Christ; and then, because there, potentially at least, in the soul of every man. God wants to be known by man, he is not happy in this state of being an unknown power, moving us from without, we know not how or why. He wants to become known in us, and to become so he must be born in us, that is, he must be in us in such a way that we become aware of him in us. This is the meaning of the transition from Job to Jesus Christ, and that further incarnation in ordinary life of which Jung writes in *Answer to Job.*

> Charles B. Hanna
> *The Face of the Deep* (pp. 144-146)

LAUGHING WITH GOD

Why do we pray or why do we fast or do our work withal, I say, so that God may be born in our souls. What were the scriptures written for and why did God create the world and the angelic nature? Simply that God might be born in the soul.

- - - - - -

The birth is not over till thy heart is free from care.

- - - - - -

Verily I say, the soul will bring forth Person if God laughs into her and she laughs back to him.

> Meister Eckhart
> *Meister Eckhart* (pp. 80,34,59)

KNOWING THE FULLNESS OF GOD

For this reason I bow my knees before the Father, from whom every family in heaven and on earth is named, that according to the riches of his glory he may grant you to be strengthened with might through his Spirit in the inner man, and that Christ may dwell in your hearts through faith; that you, being rooted and grounded in love, may have power to comprehend with all the saints what is the breadth and length and height and depth, and to know the love of Christ which surpasses knowledge, that you may be filled with all the fullness of God.

Ephesians 3:14-19, *RSV*

ABIDING IN GOD

"I am the true vine, and my Father is the vinedresser. Every branch of mine that bears no fruit, he takes away, and every branch that does bear fruit he prunes, that it may bear more fruit. You are already made clean by the word which I have spoken to you. Abide in me, and I in you. As the branch cannot bear fruit by itself, unless it abides in the vine, neither can you, unless you abide in me. I am the vine, you are the branches. He who abides in me, and I in him, he it is that bears much fruit, for apart from me you can do nothing."

John 15: 1-5, *RSV*

DESIRING GOD

So be very careful how you spend time. There is nothing more precious. In the twinkling of an eye heaven may be won or lost. God shows that time is precious, for he never gives two moments of time side by side, but always in succession.

- - - - - -

But now you will ask me, "How am I to think of God himself, and what is he?" and I cannot answer you except to say "I do not know!" For with this question you have brought me into the same darkness, the same cloud of unknowing where I want you to be! For though we through the grace of God can know fully about all other matters, and think about them — yes, even the very works of God himself — yet of God himself can no man think. Therefore I will leave on one side everything I can think, and choose for my love that thing which I cannot think! Why? Because he may well be loved, but not thought. By love he can be caught and held, but by thinking never. Therefore, though it may be good sometimes to think particularly about God's kindness and worth, and though it may be enlightening too, and a part of contemplation, yet in the work now before us it must be put down and covered with a cloud of forgetting. And you are to step over it resolutely and eagerly, with a devout and kindling love, and try to penetrate that darkness above you. Strike that thick cloud of unknowing with the sharp dart of longing love, and on no account whatever think of giving up.

- - - - - -

So when you feel by the grace of God that he is calling you to this work, and you intend to respond, lift your heart to God with humble love. And really mean God himself who created you, and bought you, and graciously called you to this state of life. And think no other thought of him. It all depends on your desire. A naked intention directed to God, and himself alone, is wholly sufficient.

If you want this intention summed up in a word, to retain it more easily, take a short word, preferably of one syllable to do so. The shorter the word the better, being more like the working of the Spirit. A word like 'GOD' or 'LOVE'. Choose which you like, or perhaps some other, so long as it is of one syllable. And fix this word fast to your heart, so that it is always there come what may. It will be your shield and your spear in peace and war alike. With this word you will hammer the cloud and the darkness above you. With this word you will suppress all thought under the cloud of forgetting. So much so that if ever you are tempted to think what it is that you are seeking, this one word will be sufficient answer. And if you would go on to think learnedly about the significance and analysis of that same word, tell yourself that you will have it whole, and not in bits and pieces. If you hold fast, that thought will surely go. And the reason? Because you refuse to let it feed on the helpful meditations we spoke of earlier.

The Cloud of Unknowing
(pp. 55- 56, 59-60, 61-62)

CONTEMPLATION: EXPERIENCE OR ESCAPE?

But in this inner world, as in the outer, the adventurer who travels without knowledge or experience or true seriousness of purpose goes forward only to his own undoing. For nature knows no pity. If one goes to the polar regions without due preparation, merely to escape from some difficulty in life, he will inevitably meet with a most unpleasant awakening. In just the same way, if one seeks the inner world in order to escape from life's tasks he will without doubt be overwhelmed and will perish. A similar fate will overtake anyone who chooses a religious life of contemplation as a means of escape from life's tasks. It is the purpose that counts. For instance, to take up the religious life of contemplation as a means of escape from life's burdens is not to experience God, but rather to fall into the unconscious and gradually be swallowed up. The visions or fantasies that come to such a man will be of a very different character from those of the true mystic and will not stand the test of analysis. The Church has always been careful to differentiate between the two and to warn against false religious experiences.

M. Esther Harding
The Way of All Women
(pp. 42- 43)

THE INWARD TRUTH OF THINGS

The action of creative faith, if it is sustained in the face of all that would deny and thwart it, will cleanse us in the process of changing and transforming us. But to be cleansed of what is unreal or perverse in thought, feeling and will is inevitably a testing experience and generally the trial is prolonged and often marked by unexpected and what may seem undeserved setbacks. That, however, is true of every vital and authentic commitment.

- - - - - -

And what sustains the soul, dedicated to discovering and living its own truth, and helps us to bear the aches and toils and hazards of the way, is the inward sense, slight and variable as it may often be at first, of being in intimate touch with Something infinitely more real than our harassed personality. There are still the stresses on the surface. Indeed they may well seem to have been intensified. But now, by this act of unwilful faith, we are aware of being related to a mysterious Power which comprehends and can reconcile in Itself all the diverse forces which still dispute for sovereignty over our outer nature. In other words we have acknowledged the basic ground of our being in which our divided faculties can find their common root and enter into concord. And through doing this we begin to see and love the inward truth of things, which does not depend on what the outer senses tell us but illuminates them.

Hugh L'Anson Fausset
Fruits of Silence (pp. 108-109)

THE ABSENCE OF GOD

By "inner" I mean our way of seeing the external world and all those realities that have no "external," "objective" presence — imagination, dreams, fantasies, trances, the realities of contemplative and meditative states, realities of which modern man, for the most part, has not the slightest direct awareness.

For example, nowhere in the Bible is there any argument about the *existence* of gods, demons, angels. People did not first "believe in" God: they experienced His presence, as was true of other spiritual agencies. The question was not whether God existed, but whether this particular God was the greatest god of all, or the only God; and what was the relation of the various spiritual agencies to each other. Today, there is a public debate, not as to the trustworthiness of God, the particular place in spiritual hierarchy of different spirits, etc., but whether God or such spirits *even exist* or ever have existed.

- - - - - -

There is no doubt, it seems to me, that there have been profound changes in the experience of man in the last thousand years. In some ways this is more evident than changes in the patterns of his behavior. There is everything to suggest that man experienced God. Faith was never a matter of believing He existed, but of trusting in the presence that was experienced and known to exist as a self-validating datum. It seems likely that far more people in our time experience neither the presence of God, nor the presence of his absence, but the absence of his presence.

R.D. Laing
The Politics of Experience
(pp. 98,100)

THE SPIRIT OF CONTEMPLATION

Contemplation is essentially a listening in silence, an expectancy. And yet in a certain sense, we must truly begin to hear God when we have ceased to listen. What is the explanation of this paradox? Perhaps only that there is a higher kind of listening, which is not an attentiveness to some special wave length, a receptivity to a certain kind of message, but a general emptiness that waits to realize the fullness of the message of God within its own apparent void. In other words, the true contemplative is not the one who prepares his mind for a particular message that he wants or expects to hear, but who remains empty because he knows that he can never expect or anticipate the word that will transform his darkness into light. He does not even anticipate a special kind of transformation. He does not demand light instead of darkness. He waits on the Word of God in silence, and when he is "answered," it is not so much by a word that bursts into his silence. It is by his silence itself suddenly, inexplicably revealing itself to him as a word of great power, full of the voice of God.

- - - - - -

Real contemplatives will always be rare and few. But that is not a matter of importance, as long as the whole Church is predominantly contemplative in all her teaching, all her activity and all her prayer. There is no contradiction between action and contemplation when Christian apostolic activity is raised to the level of pure charity. On that level, action and contemplation are fused into one entity by the love of God and of our brother in Christ. But the trouble is that if prayer is not itself deep, powerful and pure and filled at all times with the spirit of contemplation, Christian action can never really reach this high level.

Without the spirit of contemplation in all our worship — that is to say without the adoration and love of God above all, for his own sake, because he is God — the liturgy will not nourish a really Christian apostolate based on Christ's love and carried out in the power of the *Pneuma*.

The most important need in the Christian world today is this inner truth nourished by this Spirit of contemplation: the praise and love of God, the longing for the coming of Christ, the thirst for the manifestation of God's glory, his truth, his justice, his Kingdom in the world. These are all characteristically "contemplative" and eschatological aspirations of the Christian heart, and they are the very essence of monastic prayer. Without them our apostolate is more for our own glory than for the glory of God.

Without this contemplative orientation we are building churches

not to praise him but to establish more firmly the social structures, values and benefits that we presently enjoy. Without this
contemplative basis to our preaching, our apostolate is no apostolate at all, but more proselytizing to insure universal conformity
with our own national way of life.

Without contemplation and interior prayer the Church cannot
fulfill her mission to transform and save mankind. Without contemplation, she will be reduced to being the servant of cynical
and worldly powers, no matter how hard her faithful may protest
that they are fighting for the Kingdom of God.

Without true, deep contemplative aspirations, without a total
love for God and an uncompromising thirst for his truth, religion
tends in the end to become an opiate.

Thomas Merton
Contemplative Prayer
(pp. 112-113, 143-144)

DANGER

Jesus said,
The one who is near me
is near the fire
and he who is far from me
is far from the kingdom.

The Gospel According to Thomas,
Logion 82

THE SAINT

We walked towards the Piatza Romana. My teeth were gritty
with dust. I spat and said:

"It'll be a pity if they kill or injure him. He's a saint. That's
what I think."

Christian laughed, with his hands in the pockets of his over-
coat. "I'd never use that word of anyone," he said.

"All the same, it's what you think, isn't it, when you think of him?"

"We should all be able to believe that someone of our acquaintance is a saint," said Christian, evading my question. "We should be able to believe it seriously, with all the necessary critical detachment. But we should never say it. In speaking the word we debase and endanger the saints, we lead them into the temptation of pride and vanity. You may believe Sebastian to be a saint, if you can see sufficient reasons for doing so. But a saint who is publicly declared to be a saint, and does not instantly go into hiding, may very rapidly become a devil. We must await his death, to see him in the moment of supreme trial, and only then proclaim him a saint when we can no longer harm him."

He looked quizzically at me, as he had looked at Mr. Martin.

"It's right that it should be like that. The highest level of the human condition should be attained only at the highest price. Otherwise saints would be forced to make pilgrimages: they would be surrounded by press and television reporters, and politicians anxious to make use of them. In this country an accredited saint would be made a member of the National Committee, the National Assembly and the Partisans of Peace, and decorated with the Order of Labour. In the West he would do commercials for a brand of toothpaste or one of the established religions, and he'd embrace film-stars, both looking into the camera. Well, I ask you! It's better to let him pay the price. Ecstasy has to be paid for by humiliation, prison, ill-usage, public repudiation and contempt, and denial by the disciples. It is right that it should be so: it is a part of the mechanism of destiny. The greater the victory the higher the price. And there can be no cheating, because the false saint knows that he is not a saint. He knows that from the moment when he thinks of himself as a saint, instead of being concentrated upon his objective, always outside himself, he falls — and he falls lower than other men. Sainthood is the most harsh and difficult career in the world."

"The existence of a man like that is very important for the rest of us," I murmured.

"Of course," said Christian in an irritated tone. "Of course.

And he's not the only one. They're more numerous than one would believe — if one had any ideas on the subject, which one hasn't, and so much the better. It is through them that mankind as a whole, you and I, are justified and redeemed. For we are animals of the same species. Certainly a mutation has taken place in them, but they're still human beings. We can't all be like them. Or we don't want to be. But the very fact of their existence, and our ability to recognize them for what they are, is the basic compensation. Thanks to them we know that *the thing can be done,* and because of this the whole structure of the world is changed. Or rather, the world is given a structure, instead of being just a cybernetical brothel or a physio-chemical, biological, socio-historical mish-mash. It is given a meaning, a top and a bottom, and a middle layer, which is where we are. This represents an enormous consolation and hope for all of us. Sebastian is not the son of God or miraculously born; he's not an aristocrat or a philosopher or a scientist; he's just a man who was expelled from the Party, a former militant and Security officer, a bad husband, a bad father and a bad son — even worse than I am, because our parents weren't sent to prison through my doing!" Christian uttered a forced laugh. "Anyone may say, 'If he was capable of succeeding, so am I.' When there are others like him, these mutants appearing everywhere among mankind, the world will change very considerably. Even as things are, we need not be ashamed of living in the world. We can at least say, 'Even though I personally failed, even though I did not try, mankind as a whole has succeeded in him and those like him.' "

> Petru Dumitriu
> *Incognito* (pp. 470-472)

CATCHING GLIMMERS

At its heart, religion is mysticism. Moses with his flocks in Midian, Buddha under the Bo tree, Jesus up to his knees in the water of Jordan: each of them responds to Something for which words like *shalom,* oneness, God even, are only pallid souvenirs. "I have seen things," Aquinas told a friend, "that make all my writings seem like straw." Religion as institution, ethics, dogma, ritual, scripture, social action — all of this comes later and in the long run maybe counts for less. Religions start, as Frost said poems do, with a lump in the throat, to put it mildly, or with the bush going up in flames, the rain of flowers, the dove coming down out of the sky.

As for the man in the street, wherever his own religion is a matter of more than custom it is apt to be because, however dimly, a doorway opened in the air once to him too, a word was spoken, and however shakily, he too responded. The debris of his life continues to accumulate, the Vesuvius of the years scatters its ashes deep and much gets buried alive, but even under many layers the tell-tale heart can go on beating still.

Where it beats strong, there starts pulsing out from it a kind of life that is marked by, above all things perhaps, compassion — that sometimes fatal capacity for feeling what it is like to live inside another's skin, knowing that there can never really be peace and joy for any until there is peace and joy finally for all. Where it stops beating altogether, little is left religiously speaking but a good man not perhaps in Mark Twain's "worse sense of the word" but surely in the grayest and saddest: the good man whose goodness has become cheerless and finicky, a technique for working off his own guilts, a gift with no love in it which neither deceives nor benefits any for long.

Religion as a word points to that area of human experience where in one way or another man comes upon mystery as a summons to pilgrimage; where he senses meanings no less overwhelming because they can be only hinted at in myth and ritual; where he glimpses a destination that he can never know fully until he reaches it.

We are all of us more mystics than we believe or choose to believe — life is complicated enough as it is, after all. We have seen more than we let on, even to ourselves. Through some moment of beauty or pain, some sudden turning of our lives, we catch glimmers at least of what the saints are blinded by, only then, unlike the saints we tend to go on as though nothing has happened. To go on as though something *has* happened, even though we are not sure what it was or just where we are supposed to go with it, is to enter the dimension of life that religion is a word for.

Frederick Buechner
"Summons to Pilgrimage"

BECOMING

Great Leveler of men
In whom
we all
have like stature

In whom
we become
of one race

In whom
we become
of one time

In whom
we
become

Alma Loftness

Here in time we make holiday because
the eternal birth which God the Father
bore and bears unceasingly in eternity
is now born in time, in human nature.
St. Augustine says this birth is always
happening. But if it happen not in me
what does it profit me? What matters
is that it shall happen in me.

Meister Eckhart

Meister Eckhart (p. 3)

NOTES

FOREWORD
1.   Etty Hillesum, AN INTERRUPTED LIFE — THE DIARIES OF ETTY HILLESUM, 1941-1943, translated by Arno Pomerans. (New York: Pantheon Books, a division of Random House, Inc., 1983), 151.

CONFESSING OUR HUMANITY
1.   Edward Dahlberg, "Dahlberg on Dreiser, Anderson and Dahlberg," *The New York Times Book Review* (31 January 1971):3
2.   Dietrich Bonhoeffer, LIFE TOGETHER (New York: Harper & Row, Publishers, Inc., 1954), 27.
3.   Glen Gersmehl, "The Vision of Cesar Chavez," *Christianity & Crisis* (11 January 1971).
4.   Langdon Gilkey, SHANGTUNG COMPOUND (New York: Harper & Row, Publishers, Inc., 1966).
5.   Thomas A. Harris, I'M OK, YOU'RE OK (New York: Harper & Row, Publishers, Inc., 1969), 25.
6.   Ibid., 30.
7.   Ibid., 27.

PRAYER AND A COFFEE HOUSE
1.   Thomas Kelly, "The Gathered Meeting" (Philadelphia: The Friends Tract Association, 1957), 1.
2.   George Mueller, ANSWERS TO PRAYER FROM GEORGE MUELLER'S NARRATIVES, compiled by A. E. C. Brooks (Chicago: Moody Press), 46.
3.   THE RIBBON, A CELEBRATION OF LIFE, edited by the Lark Books Staff and Marianne Philbin (Asheville, NC: Lark Books, 1985), 11-13.
4.   Brother Lawrence, HIS LETTERS AND CONVERSATIONS ON THE PRACTICE OF THE PRESENCE OF GOD (Cincinnati: Forward Movement Publications), 20.
5.   Ibid.
6.   Geoffrey Hoyland, THE USE OF SILENCE (London: The Society for Promoting Christian Knowledge, 1955).

7.   Isaiah 59:10, *The New English Bible.*
8.   Petru Dumitriu, INCOGNITO (Paris: Editions du Seuil, 1969), 70.
9.   T. S. Eliot, THE COMPLETE POEMS AND PLAYS 1909-1950 (Orlando, FL: Harcourt Brace Jovanovich, Inc., 1952), 363.
10. Christmas Humphreys, CONCENTRATION AND MEDITATION (Dorset, England: Element Books Inc., 1970), 150.
11. THE CLOUD OF UNKNOWING, translated by Clifton Wolters (London: Penguin Books, Ltd., 1961), 43.
12. Robert S. de Ropp, THE MASTER GAME (New York: Delacorte Press/ Seymour Lawrence, 1968), 49-50.
13. C. E. Bignall, FLAME IN THE HEART (London: Vincent Stuart Ltd., 1965), 10.
14. Humphreys, CONCENTRATION AND MEDITATION, 42.
15. Marie-Louise von Franz, AN INTRODUCTION TO THE INTERPRETATION OF FAIRYTALES (Dallas: Spring Publications, Inc. 1970), 11.
16. THE CLOUD OF UNKNOWING, 27.
17. Meister Eckhart, MEISTER ECKHART, VOL. I, translated by C. de B. Evans (Dorset, England: Element Books Ltd., 1956), 44.
18. Eberhard Bethge, DIETRICH BONHOEFFER: MAN OF VISION, MAN OF COURAGE (New York: Harper & Row, Publishers, Inc. 1970), 380.
19. Ibid., 381.
20. Ibid., 390.
21. THE CLOUD OF UNKNOWING, 36.
22. Evelyn Underhill, PRACTICAL MYSTICISM (New York: E. P. Dutton, 1943).

EXERCISE 3
1.   Eckhart, MEISTER ECKHART, 74.
2.   Romano Guardini, PRAYER IN PRACTICE, translated by Prince Leopold (New York: Pantheon Books, a division of Random House, Inc., 1957).
3.   M. Lietaert Peerbolte, "Meditation for School Children," *Main Currents in Modern Thought,* 24, No. 1 (Sept.-Oct. 1967).

BIBLIOGRAPHY

Bell, Martin. THE WAY OF THE WOLF. Minneapolis: Winton · Seabury Press, 1968, 1969, 1970.

Berdyaev, Nicolas. DREAM AND REALITY: AN ESSAY IN AUTOBIOGRAPHY. New York: Macmillan Publishing Company, 1951.

Bethge, Eberhard. DIETRICH BONHOEFFER: MAN OF VISION, MAN OF COURAGE. New York: Harper & Row, Publishers, Inc. 1970.

Bignall, C. E. FLAME IN THE HEART. London: Vincent Stuart Ltd., 1965.

Bonhoeffer, Dietrich. LIFE TOGETHER. Translated by John W. Doberstein. New York: Harper & Row, Publishers, Inc. 1954.

——— THE WAY TO FREEDOM. Germany: Chr. Kaiser Verlag Munchen, 1966

Buber, Martin. TALES OF THE HASIDIM: EARLY MASTERS. New York: Schocken Books Inc., 1947, 1975.

——— TALES OF THE HASIDIM: LATER MASTERS. New York: Schocken Books Inc., 1948.

——— TEN RUNGS: HASIDIC SAYINGS. New York: Schocken Books Inc., 1947.

——— THE WAY OF MAN. Secaucus, NJ: Citadel Press/Lyle Stuart, Inc., 1966.

Buechner, Frederick. "Summons to Pilgrimage." *The New York Times* (Book Review), 16 March 1969.

CLOUD OF UNKNOWING, THE. Translated by Clifton Wolters. London: Penguin Books, Ltd., 1961.

Dahlberg, Edward. "Dahlberg on Dreiser, Anderson and Dahlberg." *The New York Times* (Book Review), 31 January 1971.

Delp, Alfred, S.J. THE PRISON MEDITATIONS OF FATHER DELP. New York: Herder & Herder, 1963.

de Ropp, Robert S. THE MASTER GAME. New York: Delacorte Press/Seymour Lawrence, 1968.

de Sales, St. Francis. INTRODUCTION TO THE DEVOUT LIFE. Translated by John K. Ryan. New York: Doubleday & Company, Image Books, 1955.

Dumitriu, Petru. INCOGNITO. Paris: Editions du Seuil, 1969.

Eckhart, Meister. MEISTER ECKHART, VOL. I. Translated by C. de B. Evans. Dorset, England: Element Books Ltd., 1956.

Eiseley, Loren. THE UNEXPECTED UNIVERSE. Orlando, FL: Harcourt Brace Jovanovich, Inc. 1964.

Eliot, T.S. COLLECTED POEMS 1909-1962. Orlando, FL: Harcourt Brace Jovanovich, Inc. 1936, 1963, 1964.

——— COMPLETE POEMS AND PLAYS 1909-1950. Orlando, FL: Harcourt Brace Jovanovich, Inc., 1952.

Fausset, Hugh L'Anson. FRUITS OF SILENCE. London: Abelard-Schuman Limited, 1963.

France, Malcolm. THE PARADOX OF GUILT. Philadelphia: United Church Press, 1967.

Fromm, Erich. "The Creative Attitude." In CREATIVITY AND ITS CULTIVATION. Edited by Harold H. Anderson. New York: Harper & Row, Publishers, Inc., 1959.

Gardner, John W. SELF-RENEWAL: THE INDIVIDUAL AND THE INNOVATIVE SOCIETY. New York: The Sterling Lord Agency, 1963.

Gersmehl, Glen. "The Vision of Cesar Chavez." Christianity & Crisis, 11 January 1971.

Gide, Andre. IF IT DIE. Translated by Dorothy Bussy. New York: Random House, Inc. 1935, 1963.

Gilkey, Langdon. SHANTUNG COMPOUND. New York: Harper & Row, Publishers, Inc., 1966.

"Gospel According to Thomas, The" In SECRET SAYINGS OF THE LIVING JESUS by Ray Summers. Waco, TX: Word Books, 1968.

Guardini, Romano. PRAYER IN PRACTICE. Translated by Prince Leopold. New York: Pantheon Books, a division of Random House, Inc., 1957.

Hanna, Charles B. THE FACE OF THE DEEP. New Hope, PA: Charles B. Hanna, 1967.

Harding, M. Esther. THE "I" AND THE "NOT-I": A STUDY IN THE DEVELOPMENT OF CONSCIOUSNESS. Bollingen Series LXXIX. Princeton: Princeton University Press, 1965.

——— THE WAY OF ALL WOMEN. Rev. Ed. New York: G. P. Putnam's Sons, Jung Foundation Books, 1970.

Harris, Thomas A. I'M OK, YOU'RE OK. New York: Harper & Row, Publishers, Inc., 1969.

Heschel, Abraham, J. "Hope Through Renewal of the Self." Tempo, 15 October 1969.

Hillesum, Etty. AN INTERRUPTED LIFE – THE DIARIES OF ETTY HILLESUM, 1941 -1943 translated by Arno Pomerans. New York: Pantheon Books, a division of Random House, Inc., 1983.

Hillman, James. INSEARCH: PSYCHOLOGY AND RELIGION. Zurich: James Hillman, 1967.

——— SUICIDE AND THE SOUL. Zurich: James Hillman, 1964.

Hoyland, Geoffrey. THE USE OF SILENCE. London: The Society for Promoting Christian Knowledge (S.P.C.K.), 1955.

Humphreys, Christmas. CONCENTRATION AND MEDITATION. Dorset, England: Element Books Inc., 1970

Jacobi, Jolande. THE WAY OF INDIVIDUATION. Orlando, FL: Harcourt Brace Jovanovich, Inc., 1967.

Jung, Carl G. THE COLLECTED WORKS. Princeton: Princeton University Press, 1959-1968.

Kelly, Thomas. "The Gathered Meeting." Philadelphia: The Friends Tract Association, 1957.

Kierkegaard, Soren. PURITY OF HEART. Translated by Douglas V. Steere. New York: Harper & Row, Publishers, Inc., 1938.

Krishnamurti, Jiddu. THINK ON THESE THINGS. Edited by D. Rajagopal. New York: Harper & Row, Publishers, Inc., 1964.

Kunkel, Fritz. IN SEARCH OF MATURITY. New York: Charles Scribner's Sons, 1943.

Laing, R. D. THE POLITICS OF EXPERIENCE AND THE BIRDS OF PARADISE. London: Penguin Books Ltd., 1967.

Lawrence, Brother. HIS LETTERS AND CONVERSATIONS ON THE PRACTICE OF THE PRESENCE OF GOD. Cincinnati: Forward Movement Publications.

Loomis, Earl A., Jr. THE SELF IN PILGRIMAGE. New York: Harper & Bros., 1960.

Lynch, William F., S.J. IMAGES OF HOPE. New York: Curtis Brown Ltd., 1965.

Maslow, Abraham H. TOWARD A PSYCHOLOGY OF BEING. New York: Van Nostrand Reinhold Company, 1968.

May, Rollo. LOVE AND WILL. New York: W. W. Norton & Company, Inc., 1969.

Merton, Thomas. CONTEMPLATIVE PRAYER. New York: Doubleday & Company, Inc., 1969.

Moustakas, Clark. CREATIVITY AND CONFORMITY. New York: Van Nostrand Reinhold Company, 1967.

Mueller, George. ANSWERS TO PRAYER FROM GEORGE MUELLER'S NARRATIVES. Compiled by A. E. C. Brooks. Chicago: Moody Press.

Nouwen, Henry. "Generation without Fathers." *Commonweal,* 12 June 1970.

Oates, Wayne E. THE HOLY SPIRIT IN FIVE WORLDS. New York: Association Press, 1968.

Pascal, Blaise. PENSEES. Translation and Introduction by Martin Turnell. London: The Harvill Press, 1962.

Peerbolte, M. Lietaert. "Meditation for School Children." *Main Currents in Modern Thought,* 24, No. 1 (Sept.-Oct. 1967).

Progoff, Ira. THE SYMBOLIC AND THE REAL. New York: The Julian Press, Inc., 1963.

Proust, Marcel. REMEMBRANCE OF THINGS PAST. Translated by Moncrieff and Kilmartin. New York: Random House, Inc., 1981.

Radcliffe, Lynn J. MAKING PRAYER REAL. Nashville: Abingdon-Cokesbury Press, 1952.

Rahner, Karl. ON PRAYER. Tunbridge Wells, England: Burns & Oates Ltd., 1965.

RIBBON, THE: A CELEBRATION OF LIFE. Edited by the Lark Books Staff and Marianne Philbin. Asheville, NC: Lark Books, 1985.

Roberts, David E. PSYCHOTHERAPY AND A CHRISTIAN VIEW OF MAN. New York: Charles Scribner's Sons, 1950, 1978.

Rohrbach, Peter-Thomas, O.C.D. CONVERSATION WITH CHRIST. Rockford, IL: TAN Books & Publications, Inc., 1956.

Suzuki, Daisetz Teitaro. MYSTICISM: CHRISTIAN AND BUDDHIST. New York: Harper & Row, Publishers, Inc., 1957.

Teale, Edwin Way. NORTH WITH THE SPRING. New York: Dodd, Mead & Company, Inc. 1951.

Teresa of Avila, Saint. THE COMPLETE WORKS OF SAINT TERESA OF JESUS. Vol. I, *Life*. Translated and edited by E. Allison Peer. London: Sheed & Ward Ltd., 1949.

Thielicke, Helmut. HOW THE WORLD BEGAN. Translation and Introduction by John W. Doberstein. Philadelphia: Fortress Press, 1961.

Tozer, A. W. THE PURSUIT OF GOD. Camp Hill, PA: Christian Publications, 1948.

Underhill, Evelyn. MYSTICISM. New York: E. P. Dutton, 1961.

——— PRACTICAL MYSTICISM. New York: E. P. Dutton, 1943.

von Franz, Marie-Louise. AN INTRODUCTION TO THE INTERPRETATION OF FAIRYTALES. Dallas: Spring Publications, Inc., 1970.

Whipple, Richard O. "The View from Zorna." *Main Currents in Modern Thought,* 24, No. 1 (Sept.-Oct. 1967).

Wyon, Olive. THE SCHOOL OF PRAYER. Philadelphia: The Westminster Press, 1943.

ELIZABETH O'CONNOR

Elizabeth O'Connor has been on the staff of The Church of The Saviour, Washington, D.C., since 1953. Prior to that she worked in the field of public relations. She has participated in many of the mission programs of The Church of The Saviour and was a member of the group which brought into being The Potter's House (described in this book). The Potter's House was the first church-related coffee house in the country and is well-known throughout the world as the seedbed for innovative inner city programs. In 1984 Elizabeth O'Connor founded Sarah's Circle, an intergenerational program for elderly low-income persons in the neighborhood of The Potter's House. She has worked intensively as a group therapist and is currently using her therapeutic skills in the inner city.

In May 1984 she was awarded the degree of Doctor of Humane Letters, honoris causa, by Protestant Episcopal Theological Seminary, Alexandria, Virginia. In October 1985 she was honored by The Center for The Ministry of The Laity, Andover Newton Theological School "for her unique contribution as a writer illuminating the faith journey of Christians committed to the mission of God."

Other books by this author are: *Call to Commitment; Journey Inward, Journey Outward; Eighth Day of Creation; Our Many Selves; The New Community;* and *Letters to Scattered Pilgrims.*

LuraMedia™ PUBLICATIONS

by Pat Backman
JOURNEY WITH MATTHEW
(ISBN 0-931055-03-2)

by Marjory Zoet Bankson
BRAIDED STREAMS:
Esther and a Woman's Way
of Growing
(ISBN 0-931055-05-9)

by Lura Jane Geiger
ASTONISH ME, YAHWEH!:
Leader's Guide
(ISBN 0-931055-02-4)

**by Lura Jane Geiger
with Pat Backman**
BRAIDED STREAMS:
Leader's Guide
(ISBN 0-931055-09-1)

**by Lura Jane Geiger, Sandy Landstedt,
Mary Geckeler, and Peggie Oury**
ASTONISH ME, YAHWEH!:
A Bible Workbook-Journal
(ISBN 0-931055-01-6)

by Ted Loder
GUERRILLAS OF GRACE:
Prayers for the Battle
(ISBN 0-931055-04-0)
NO ONE BUT US:
Personal Reflections on Public Sanctuary
(ISBN 0-931055-08-3)
TRACKS IN THE STRAW:
Tales Spun from the Manger
(ISBN 0-931055-06-7)

by Elizabeth O'Connor
SEARCH FOR SILENCE
(ISBN 0-931055-07-5)

LuraMedia™ operates as a creative publishing forum. LuraMedia™ selects, designs, produces and distributes books, teaching manuals and cassette tapes with subject area specialization in personal growth using journaling, music, art, meditation, stories and creativity in a spiritual context.

LuraMedia™ is a company that searches for ways to encourage personal growth, shares the excitement of creative integrity, and believes in the power of faith to change lives.

LuraMedia™
10227 Autumnview Lane
San Diego, California 92126-0998